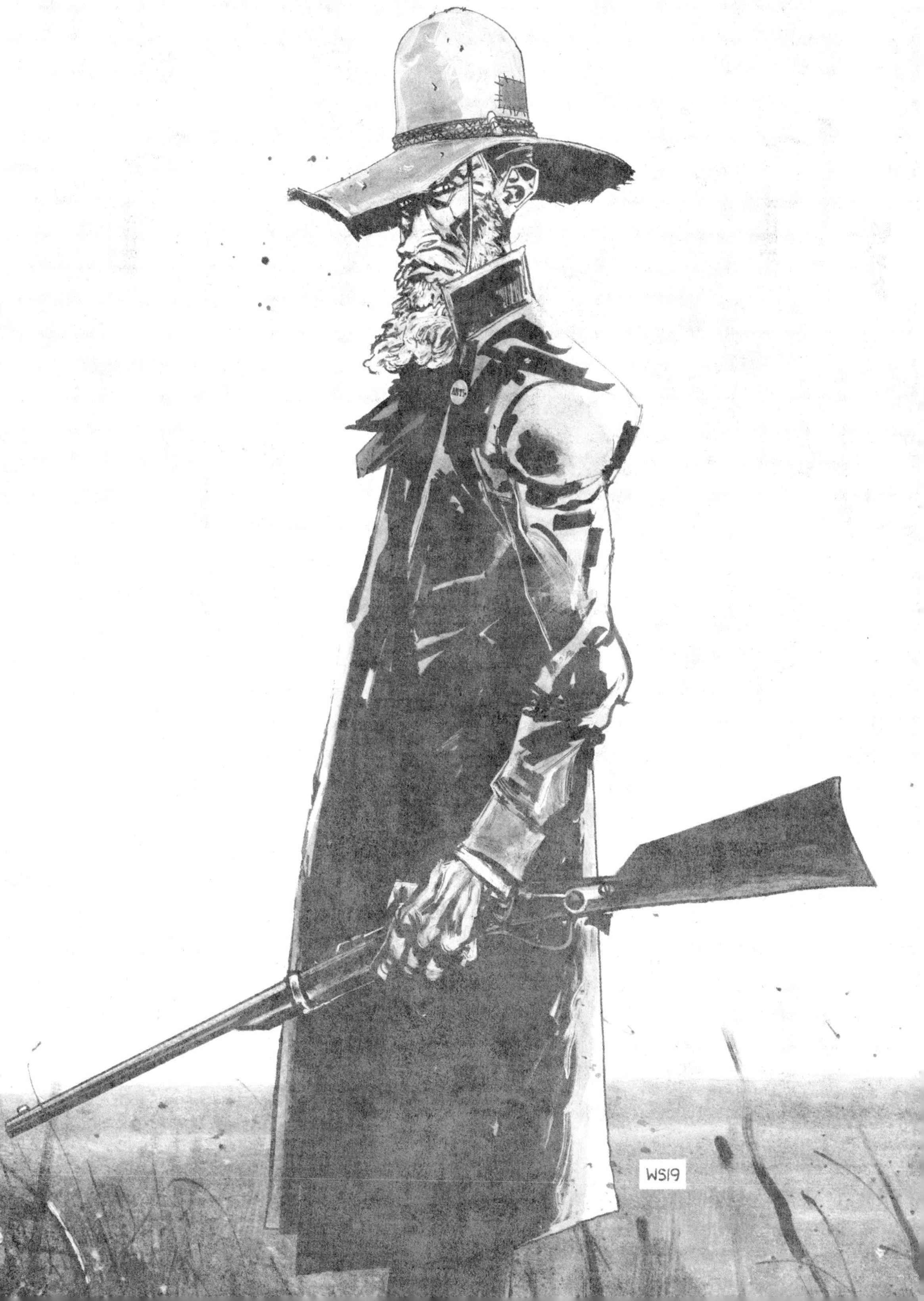
ASTA
WS19

1

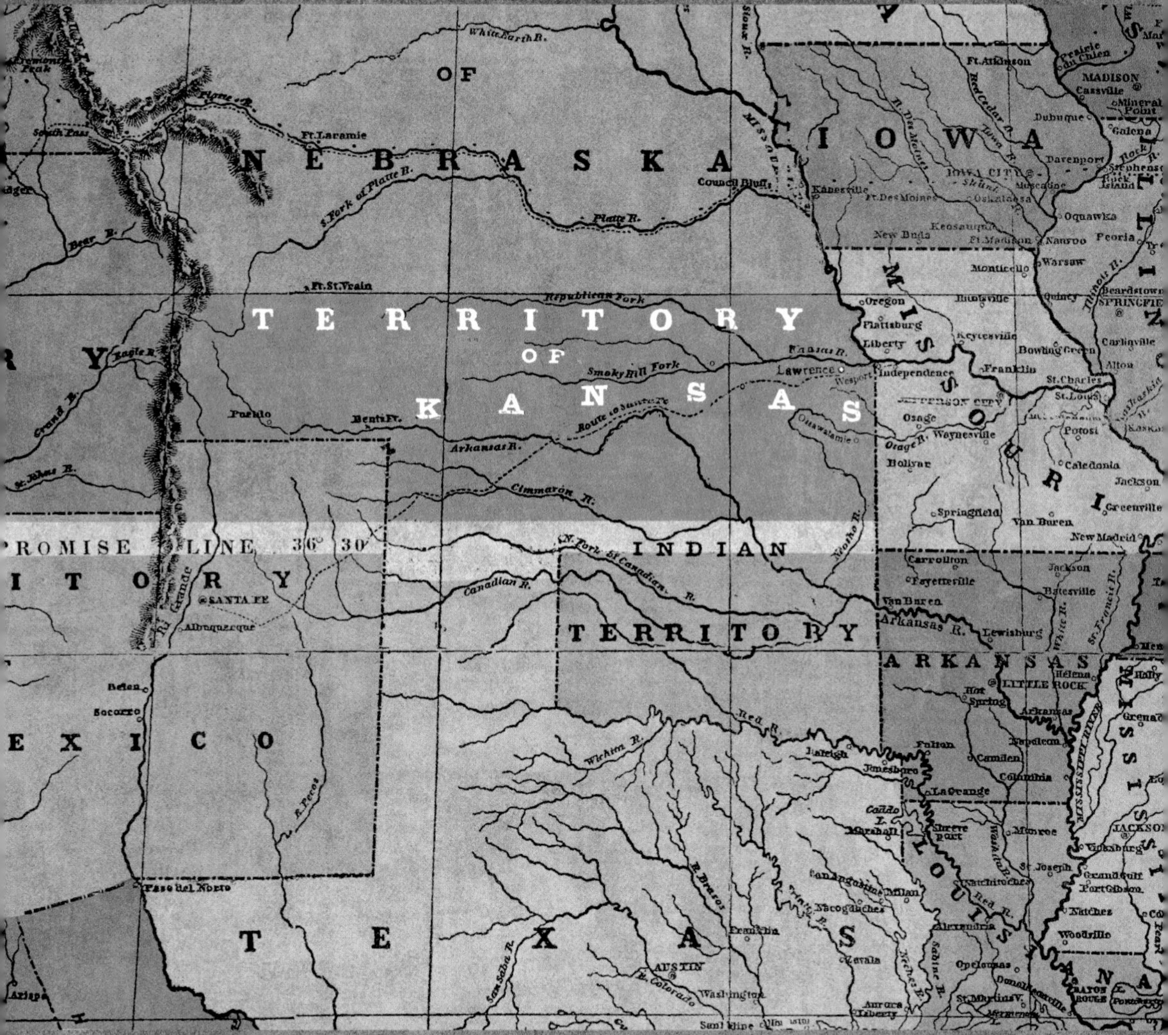

OF
NEBRASKA
TERRITORY
OF
KANSAS
INDIAN
TERRITORY
IOWA
MISSOURI
ARKANSAS
TEXAS
Ft.Laramie
Platte R.
S.Fork of Platte R.
Council Bluffs
Ft.St.Vrain
Republican Fork
Smoky Hill Fork
Kansas R.
Lawrence
Independence
Arkansas R.
Cimmaron R.
Canadian R.
Red R.
Oregon
Plattsburg
Liberty
Franklin
St.Charles
Springfield
Van Buren
Carrollton
Fayetteville
Little Rock
Fulton
Camden
LaGrange
Osage
Waynesville
Bolivar
Pueblo
Bents Ft.
SANTA FE
Albuquerque
Socorro
EXICO
ROMISE LINE 36° 30′
Davenport
Dubuque
Galena
MADISON
Oquawka
Nauvoo
Peoria
Warsaw
Quincy
Keosauqua
Ft.Madison
Ft.Atkinson
Shreve Port
Natchitoches
Alexandria
Opelousas
AUSTIN
Washington
Nacogdoches
Marshall
Monroe
Vicksburg
Natchez
Woodville
R.Pecos
R.Brazos
Trinity R.
Sabine R.
R.Colorado
Paso del Norte

As a young boy, Captain John Brown swore he'd dedicate his life to the struggle against slavery. He embarked on a mission, along with his brood and like-minded fellow Americans, to be mild with the mild, shrewd with the crafty, confiding to the honest, rough to the ruffian, and to the liar--
a **THUNDERBOLT!**

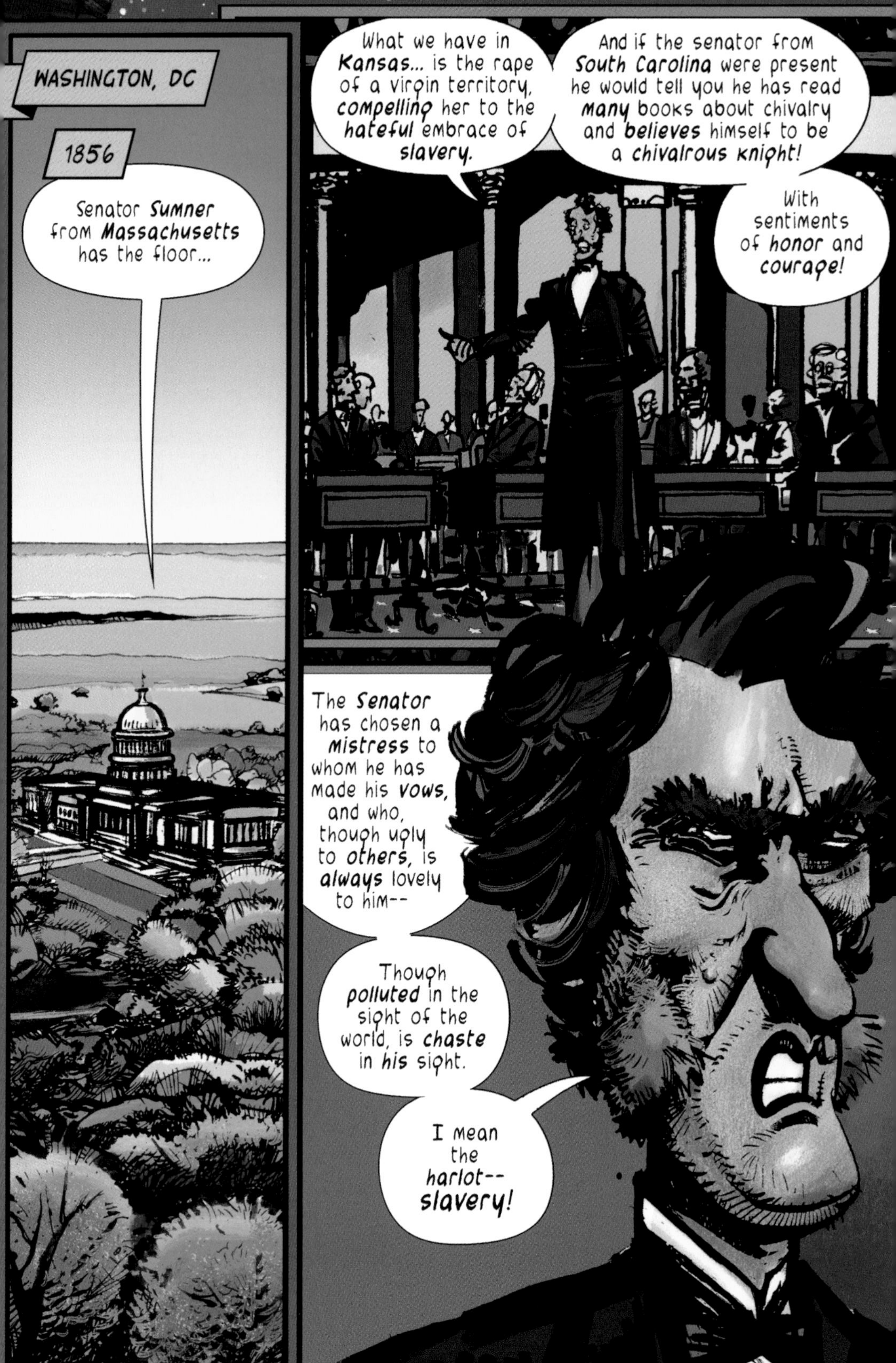
WASHINGTON, DC
1856
Senator Sumner from Massachusetts has the floor...
What we have in Kansas... is the rape of a virgin territory, compelling her to the hateful embrace of slavery.
And if the senator from South Carolina were present he would tell you he has read many books about chivalry and believes himself to be a chivalrous knight!
With sentiments of honor and courage!
The Senator has chosen a mistress to whom he has made his vows, and who, though ugly to others, is always lovely to him--
Though polluted in the sight of the world, is chaste in his sight.
I mean the harlot--slavery!

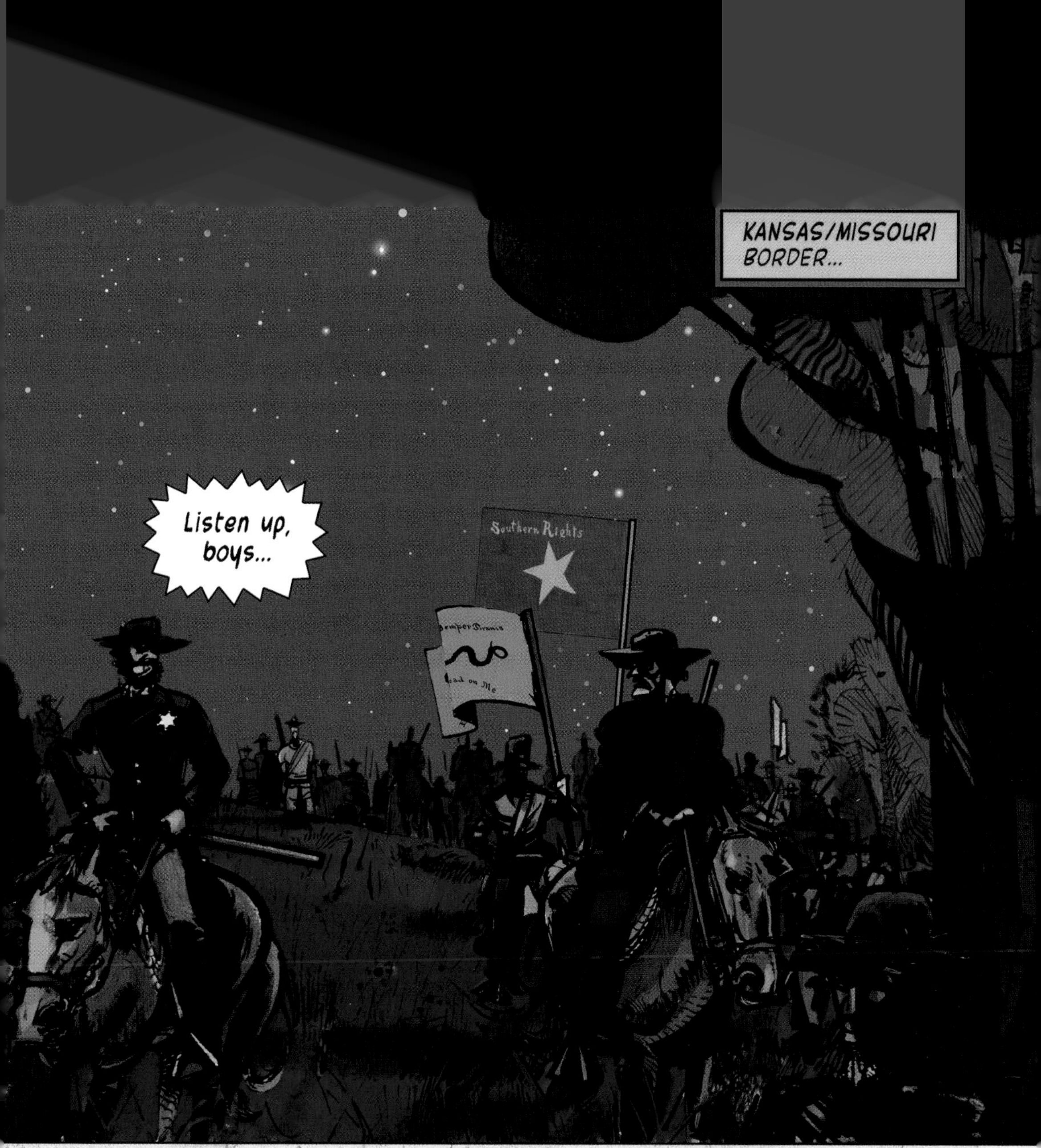
KANSAS/MISSOURI BORDER...
Listen up, boys...
Southern Rights

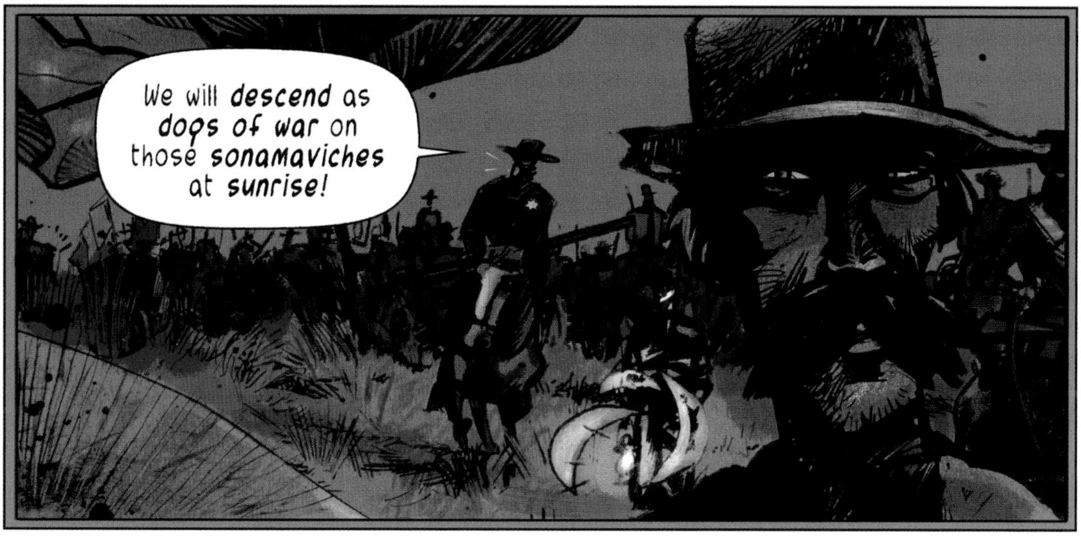
We will descend as dogs of war on those sonamaviches at sunrise!

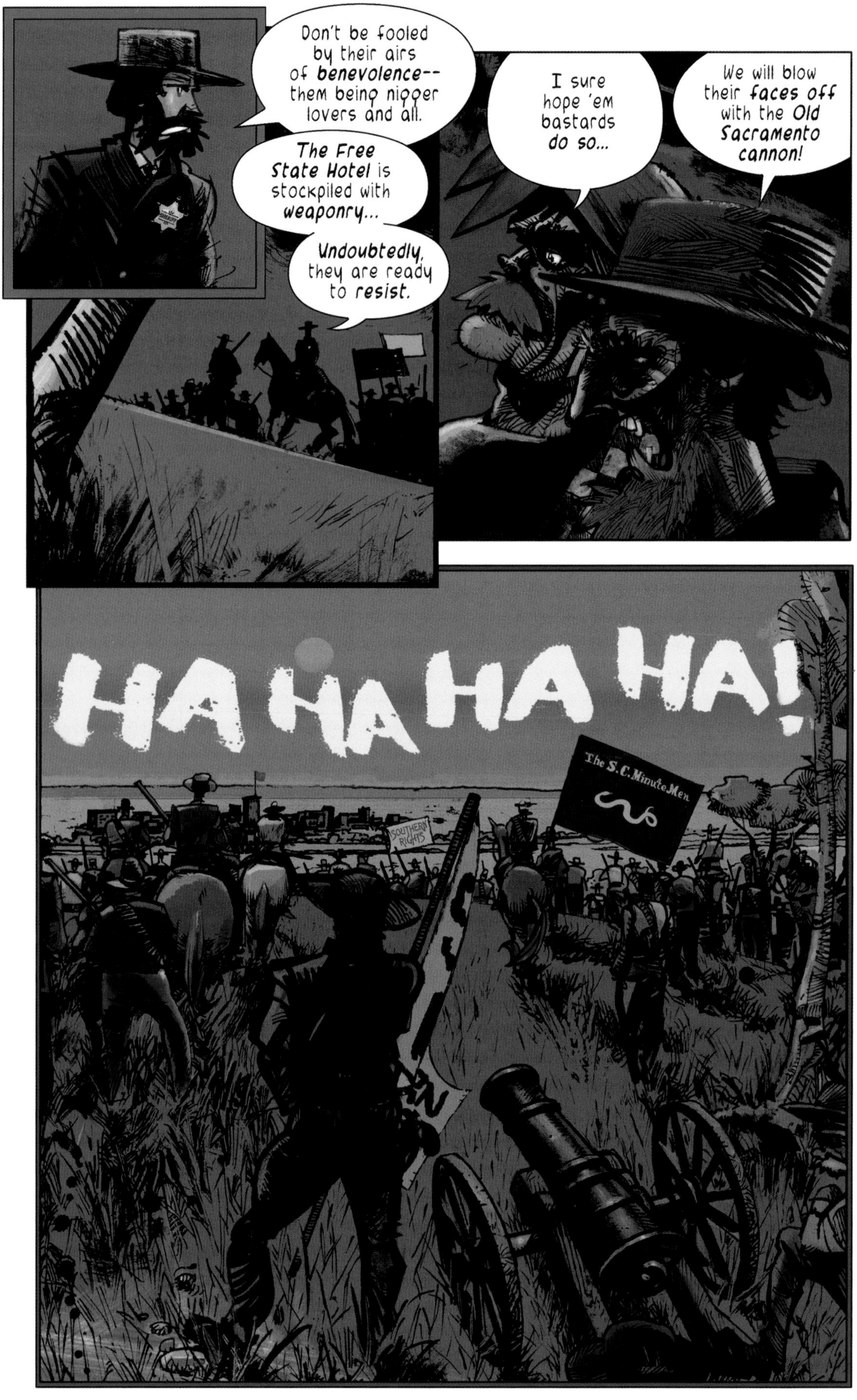

Don't be fooled by their airs of **benevolence**-- them being nigger lovers and all.
The Free State Hotel is stockpiled with ***weaponry***...
Undoubtedly, they are ready to ***resist***.
I sure hope 'em bastards *do so*...
We will blow their ***faces off*** with the ***Old Sacramento cannon!***
HA HA HA HA HA!
SOUTHERN RIGHTS
The S.C. Minute Men

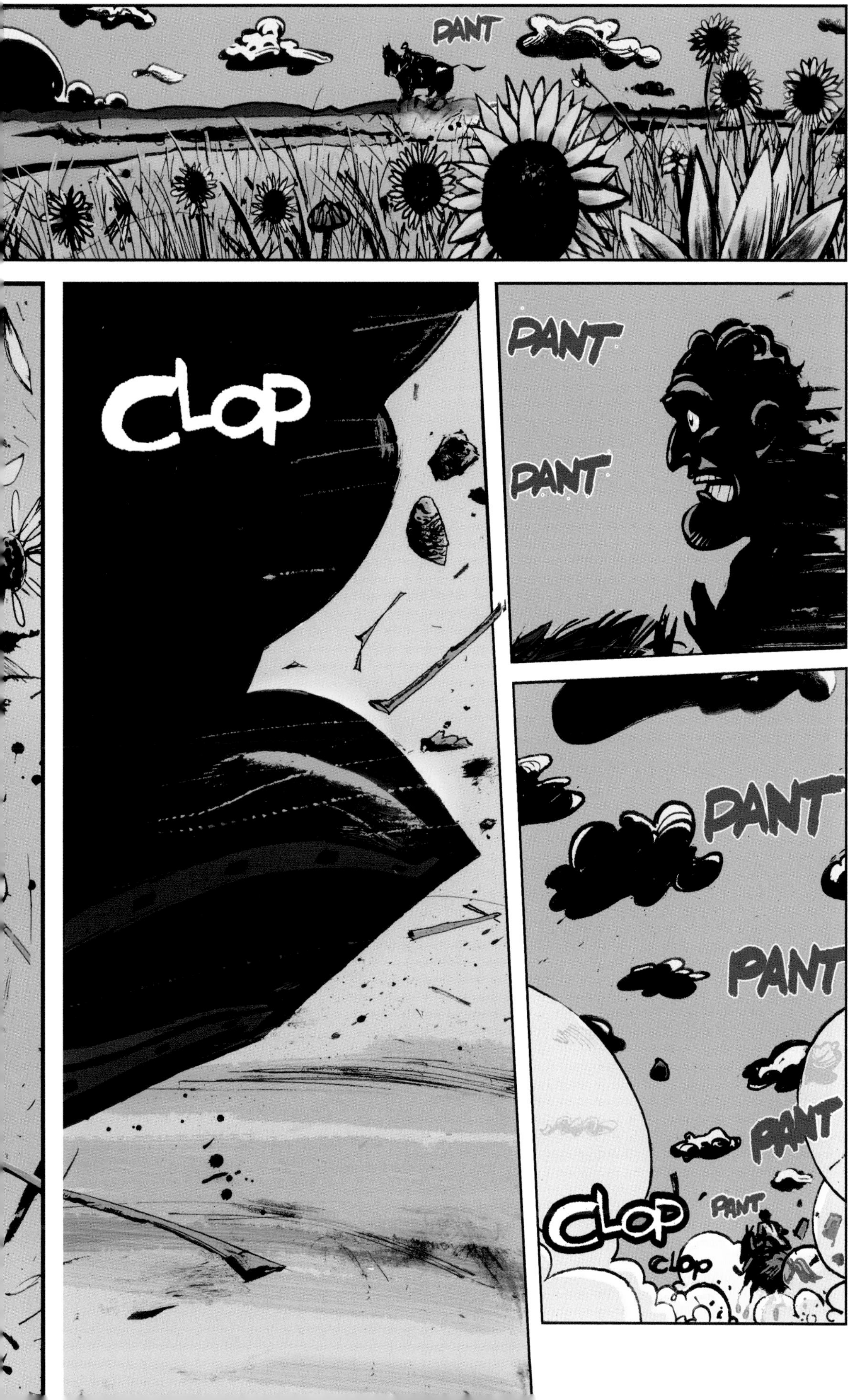
PANT
CLOP
PANT
PANT
PANT
PANT
PANT
CLOP
PANT
CLOP

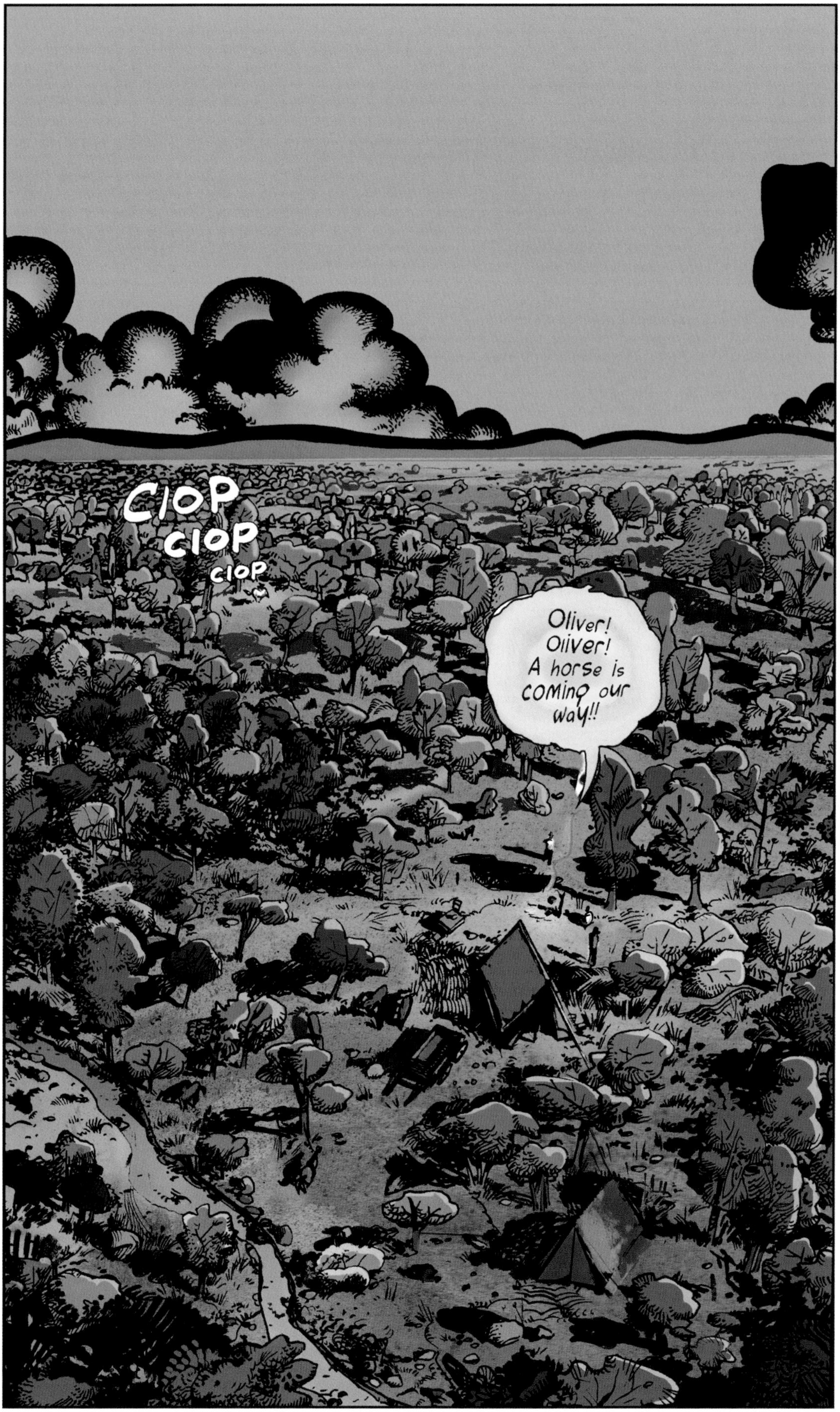
CLOP
CLOP
CLOP
Oliver! Oliver! A horse is coming our way!!

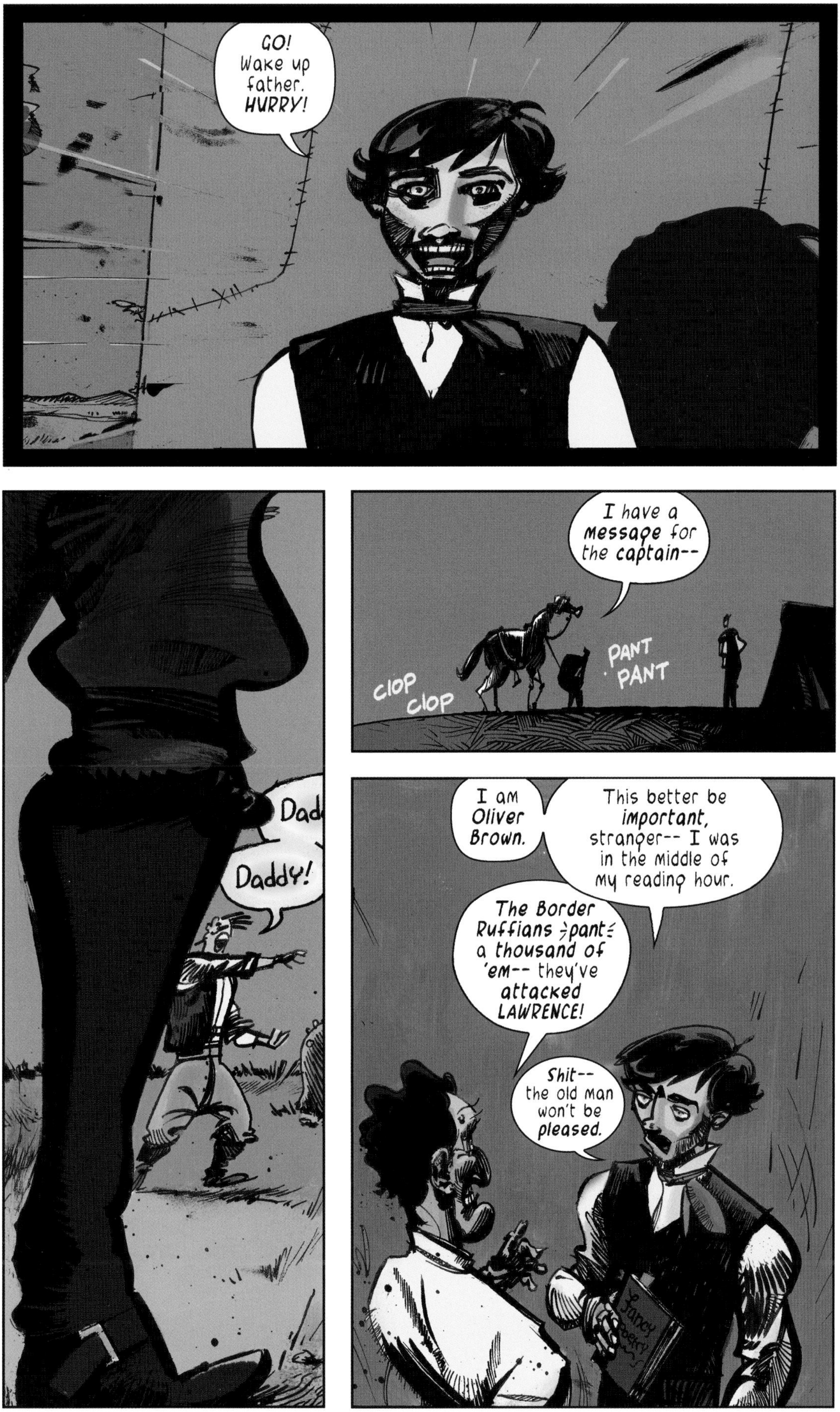

GO! Wake up father. HURRY!
Dad
Daddy!
I have a message for the captain--
CLOP CLOP
PANT PANT
I am Oliver Brown.
This better be important, stranger-- I was in the middle of my reading hour.
The Border Ruffians ≥pant≤ a thousand of 'em-- they've attacked LAWRENCE!
Shit-- the old man won't be pleased.

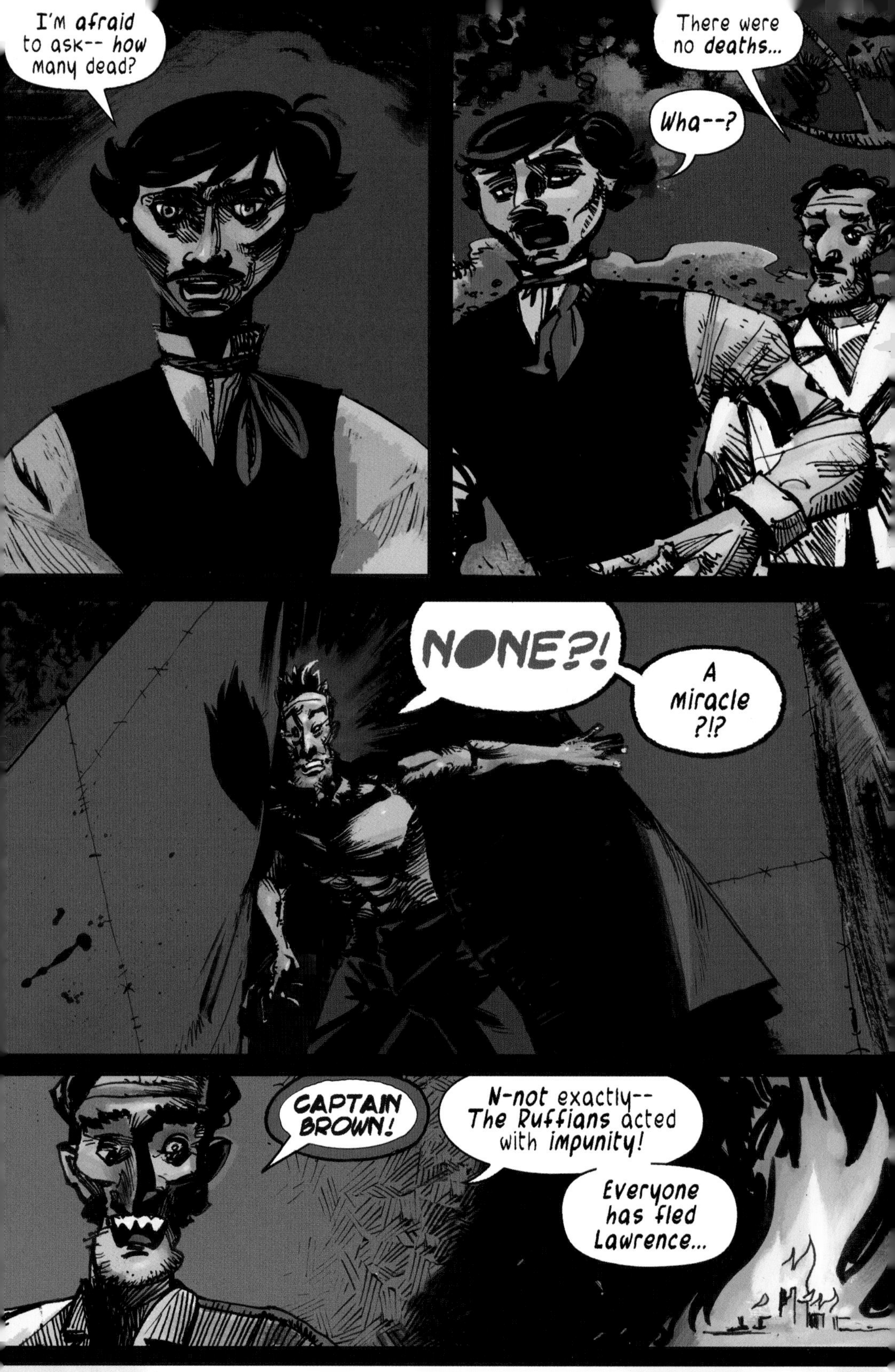

I'm afraid to ask-- how many dead?
There were no deaths...
Wha--?
NONE?!
A Miracle ?!?
CAPTAIN BROWN!
N-not exactly-- The Ruffians acted with impunity!
Everyone has fled Lawrence...

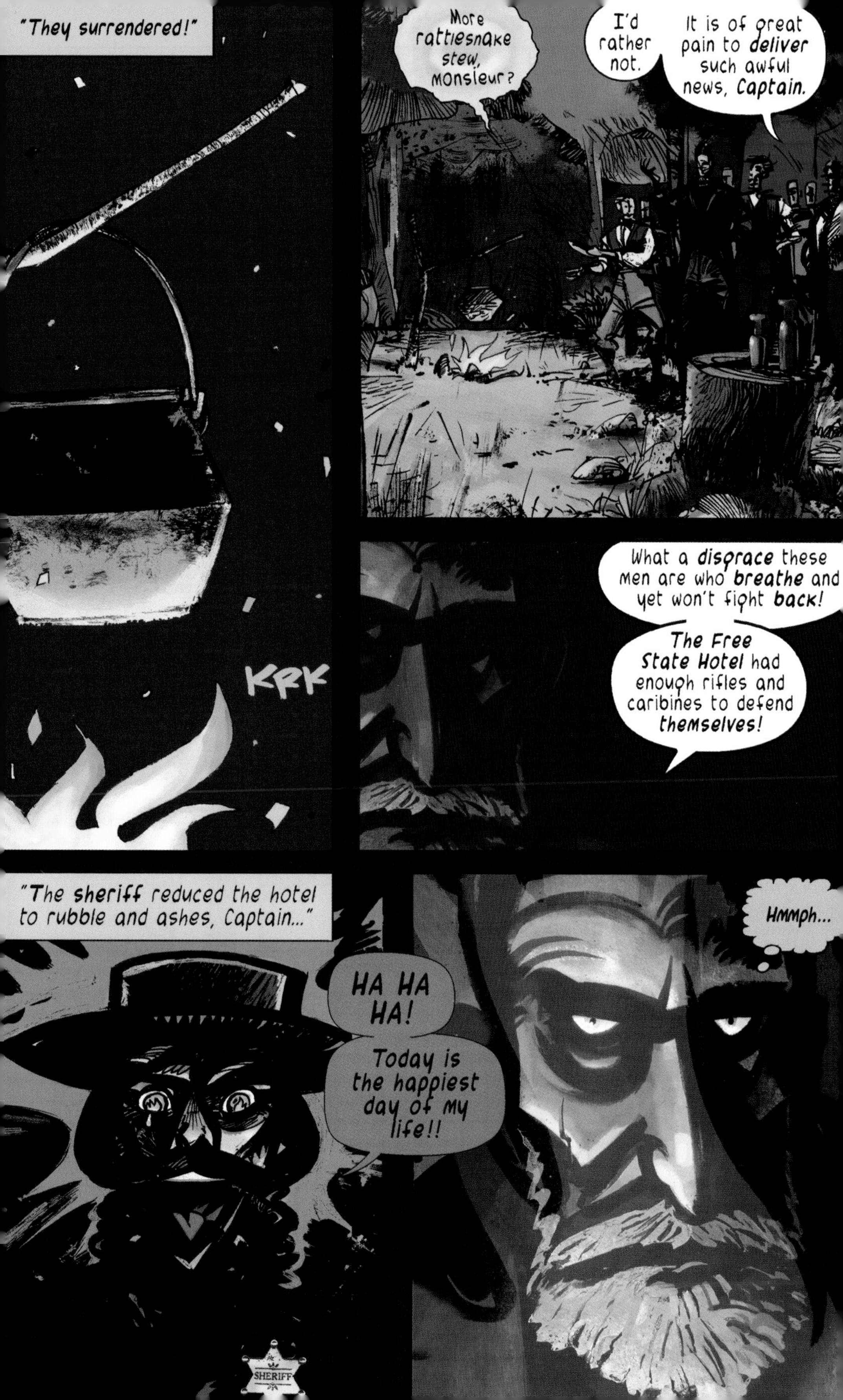
"They surrendered!"
KRK
More rattiesnake stew, monsieur?
I'd rather not.
It is of great pain to deliver such awful news, Captain.
What a disgrace these men are who breathe and yet won't fight back!
The Free State Hotel had enough rifles and caribines to defend themselves!
"The sheriff reduced the hotel to rubble and ashes, Captain..."
HA HA HA!
Today is the happiest day of my life!!
SHERIFF
Hmmph...

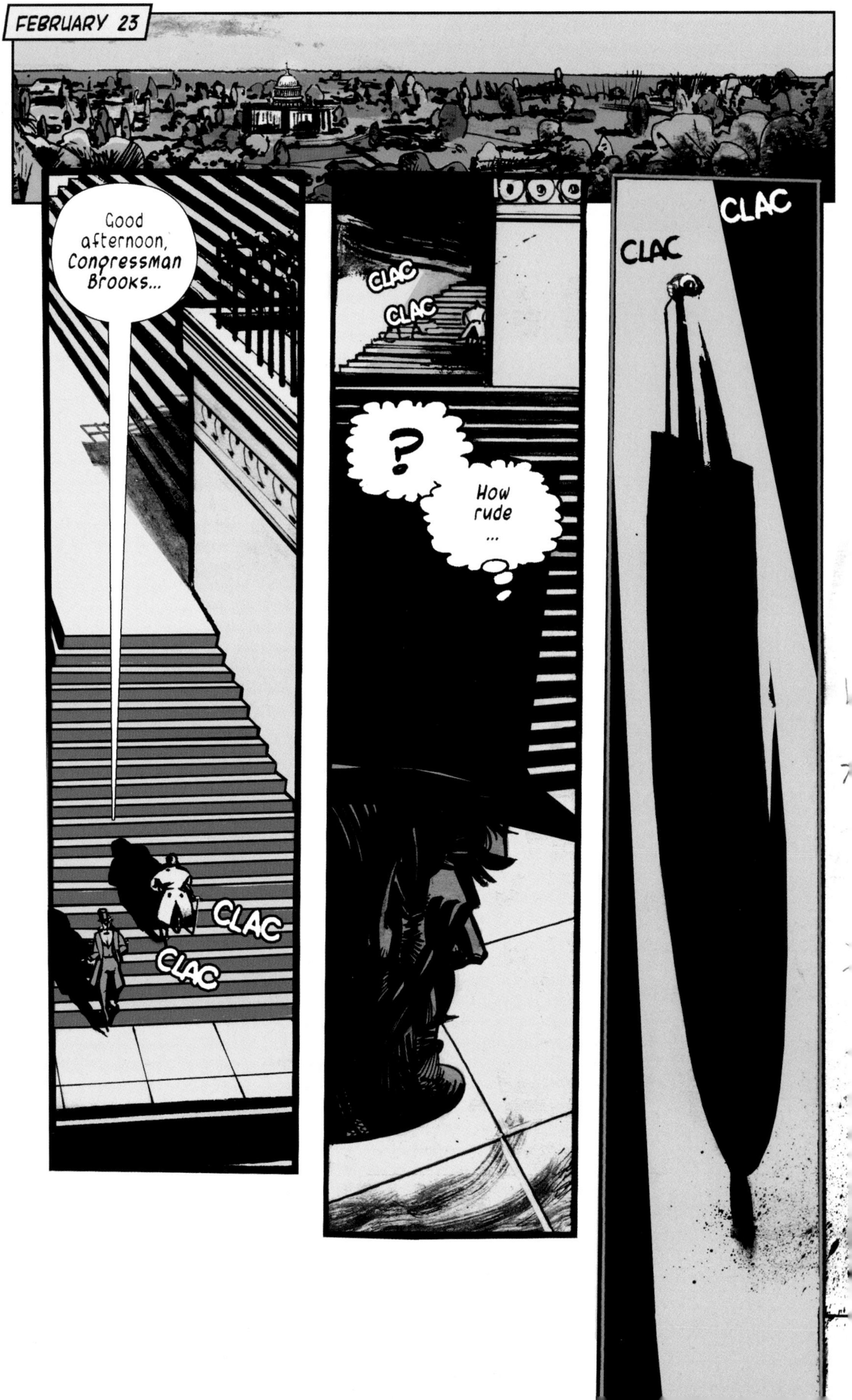
FEBRUARY 23
Good afternoon, Congressman Brooks...
CLAC
CLAC
CLAC
CLAC
?
How rude ...
CLAC
CLAC

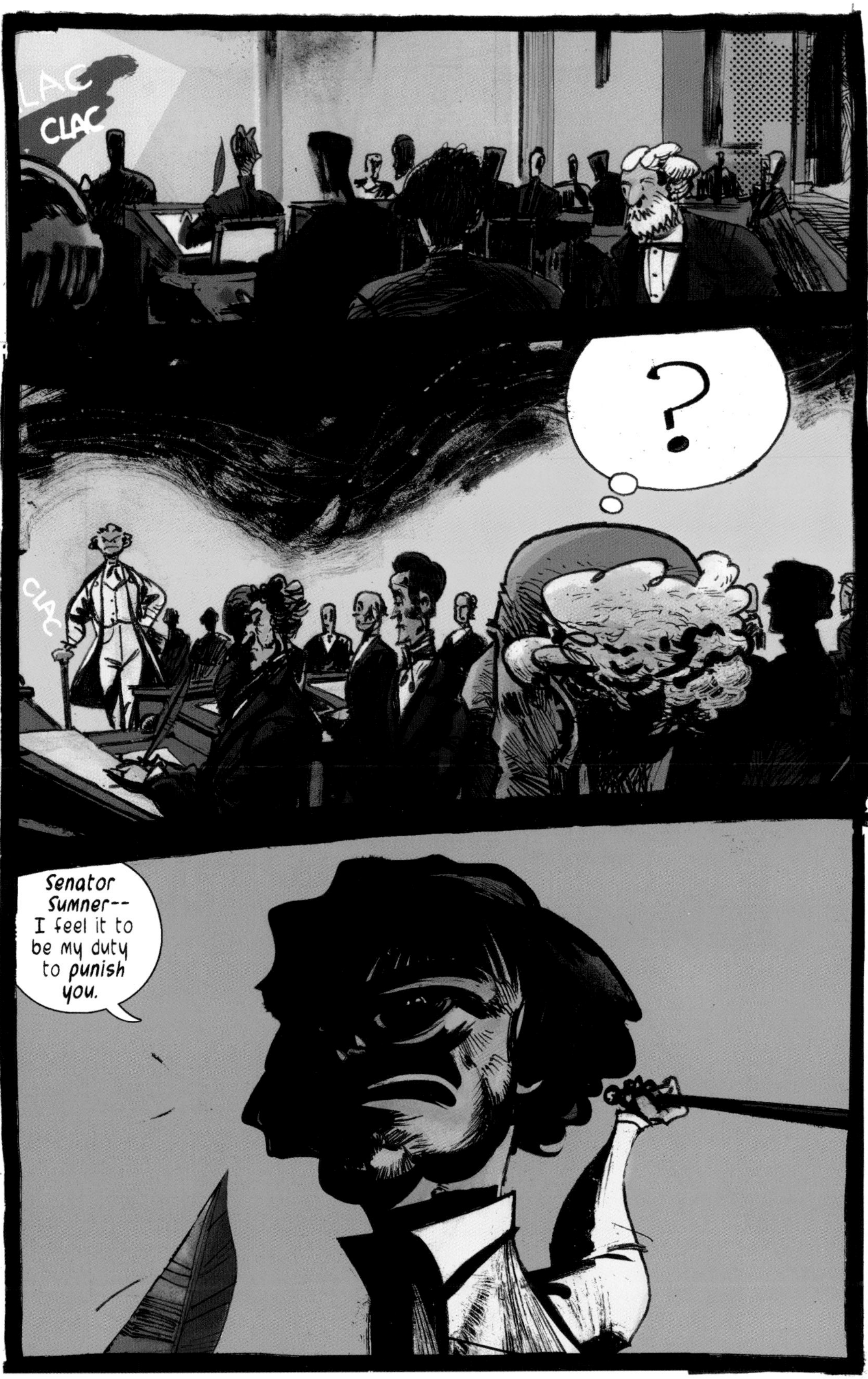
CLAC
CLAC
?
CLAC
Senator Sumner-- I feel it to be my duty to punish you.

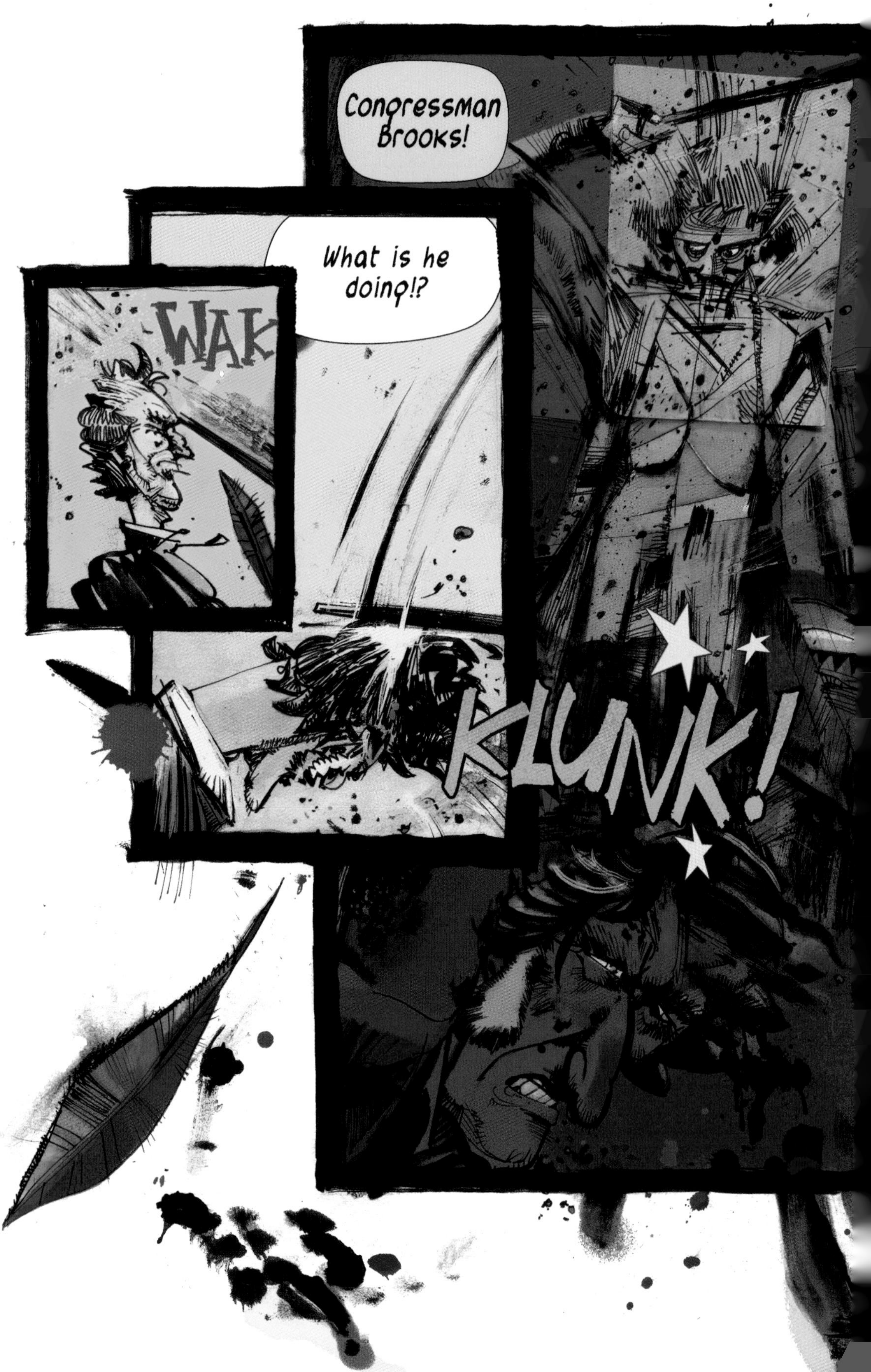
Congressman Brooks!
What is he doing!?
WAK
KLUNK!

Let him have it!
Has he gone mad?
The senator shouldn't have spoken so poorly of others!
PRtzzz
WAK
Sir Brooks is merely defending his kinsman's honor!
WAK
...Dear Lord, he has lost his marbles!
WAK
Enough Mr. Brooks
someone, please ...
WAK
Ha, ha, ha! Look at that!
WAK

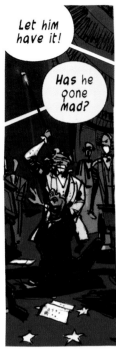

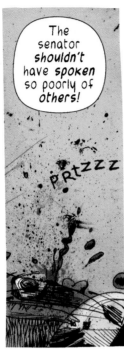

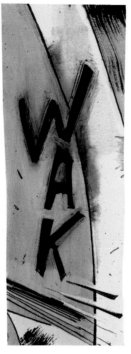

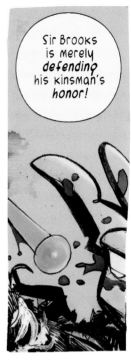

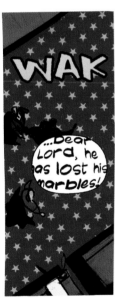

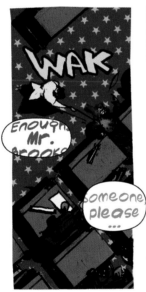

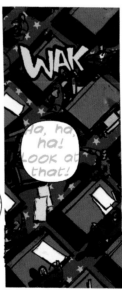

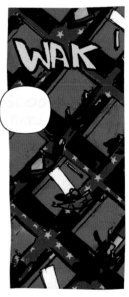

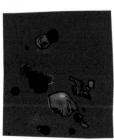

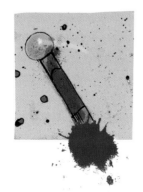

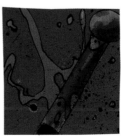

THUND

AN AMER

H 9:22

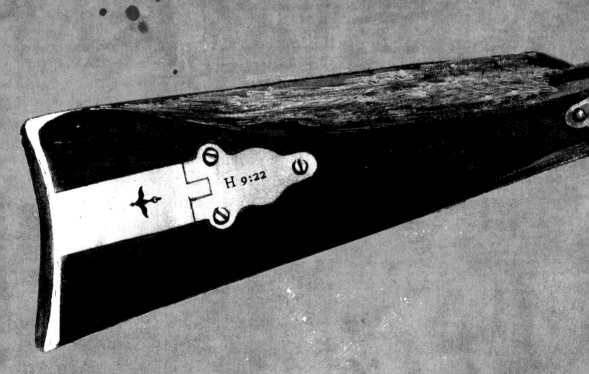

ERBOLT VOL.1

CAN TALE

WRITTEN & ILLUSTRATED BY
WILFRED SANTIAGO

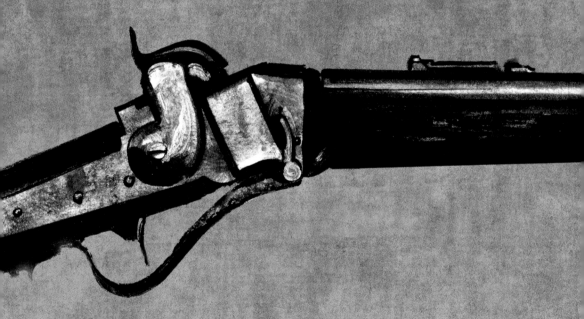

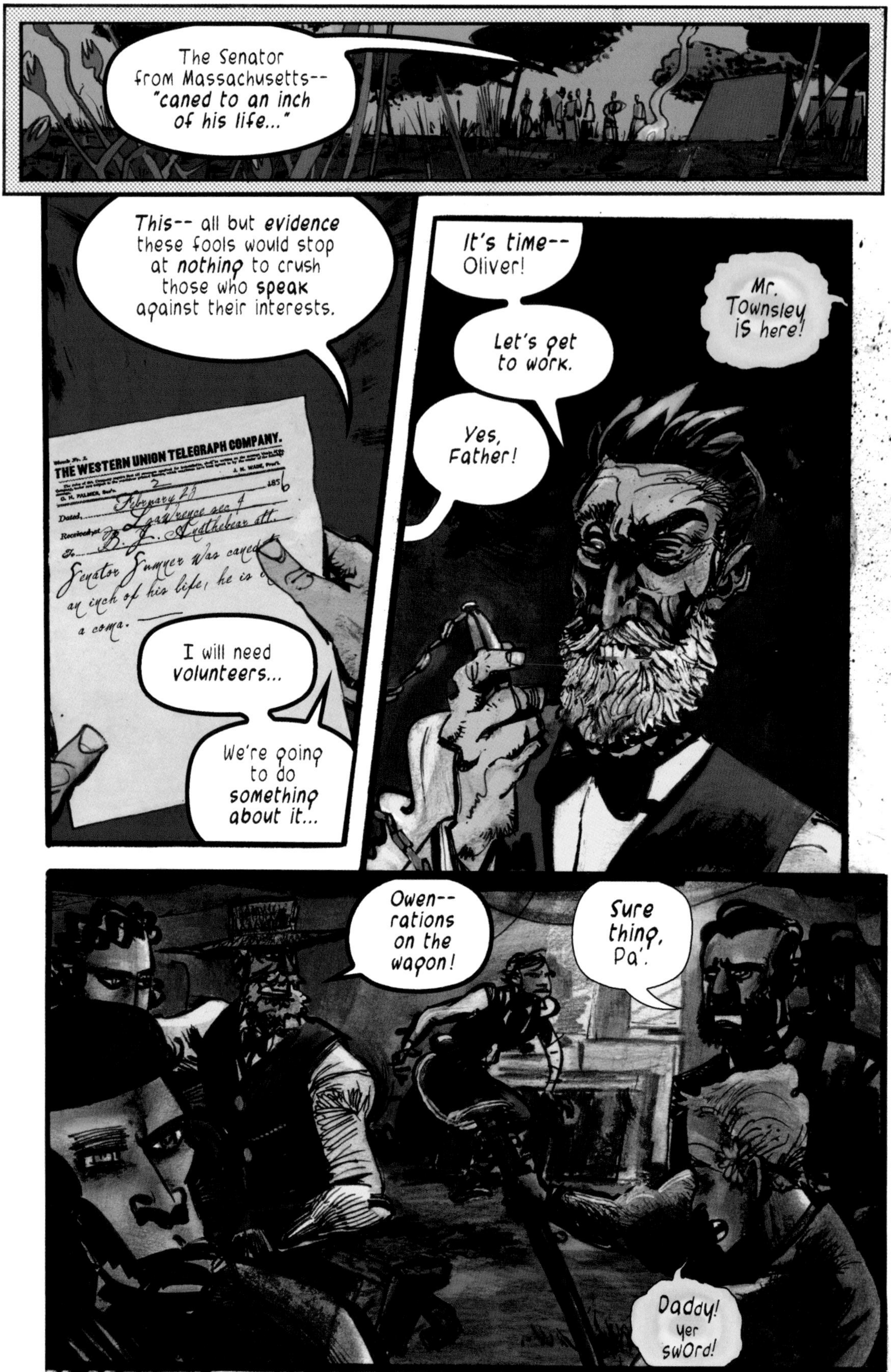
The Senator from Massachusetts-- "caned to an inch of his life..."
This-- all but evidence these fools would stop at nothing to crush those who speak against their interests.
THE WESTERN UNION TELEGRAPH COMPANY.
I will need volunteers...
We're going to do something about it...
It's time-- Oliver!
Let's get to work.
Yes, Father!
Mr. Townsley IS here!
Owen-- rations on the wagon!
Sure thing, Pa'.
Daddy! yer swOrd!

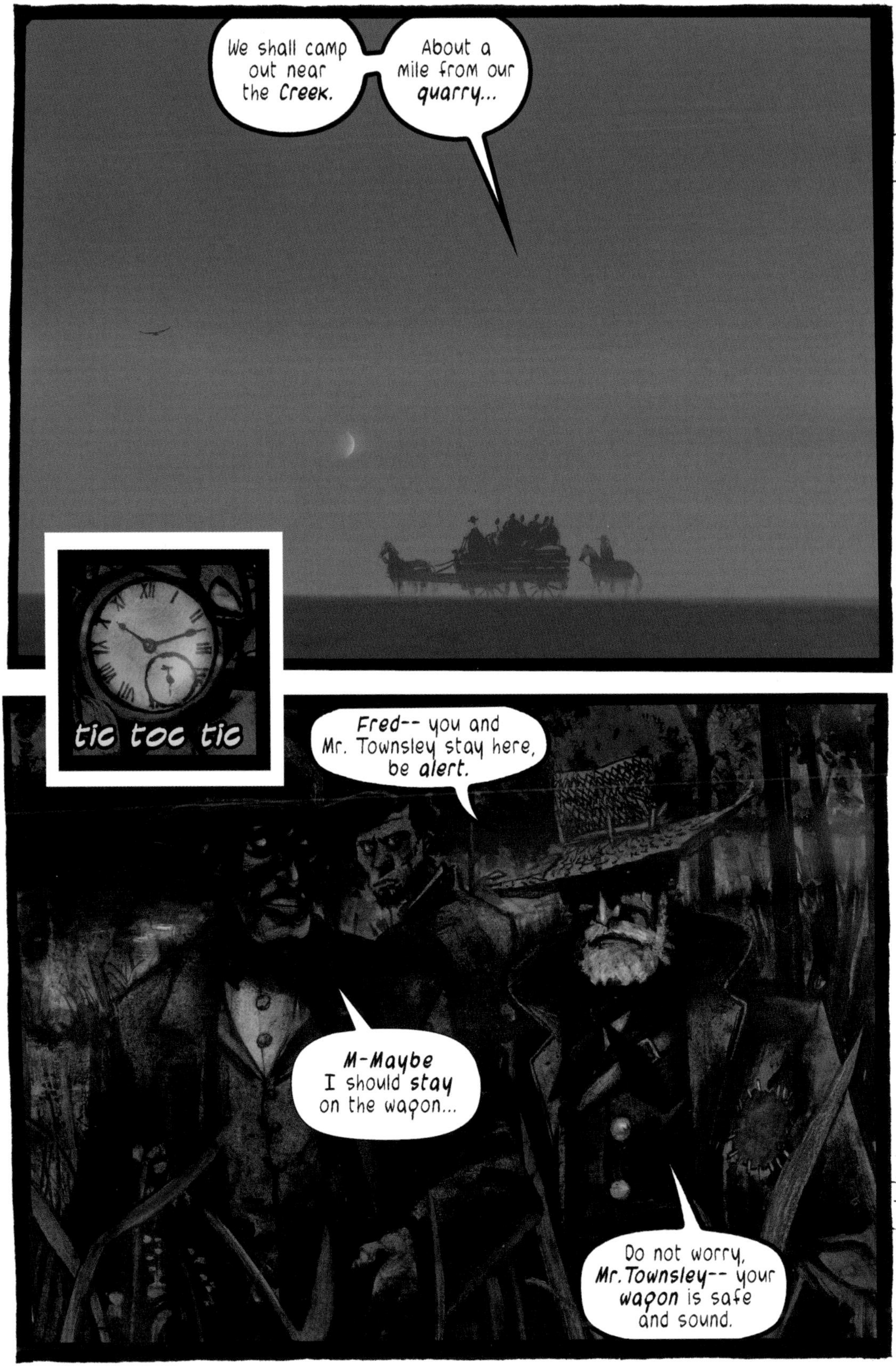
We shall camp out near the Creek.
About a mile from our quarry...
tic toc tic
Fred-- you and Mr. Townsley stay here, be alert.
M-Maybe I should stay on the wagon...
Do not worry, Mr. Townsley-- your wagon is safe and sound.

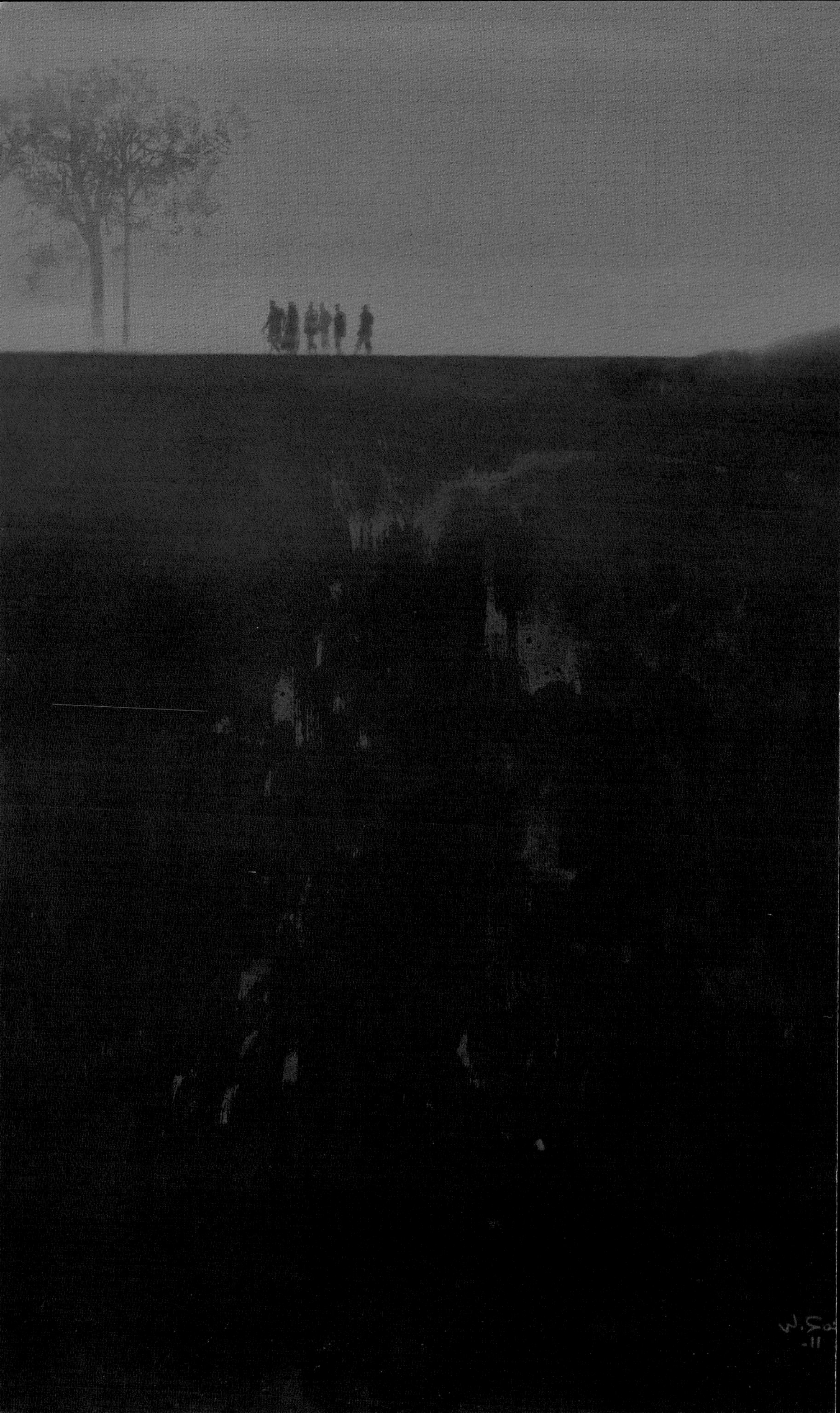

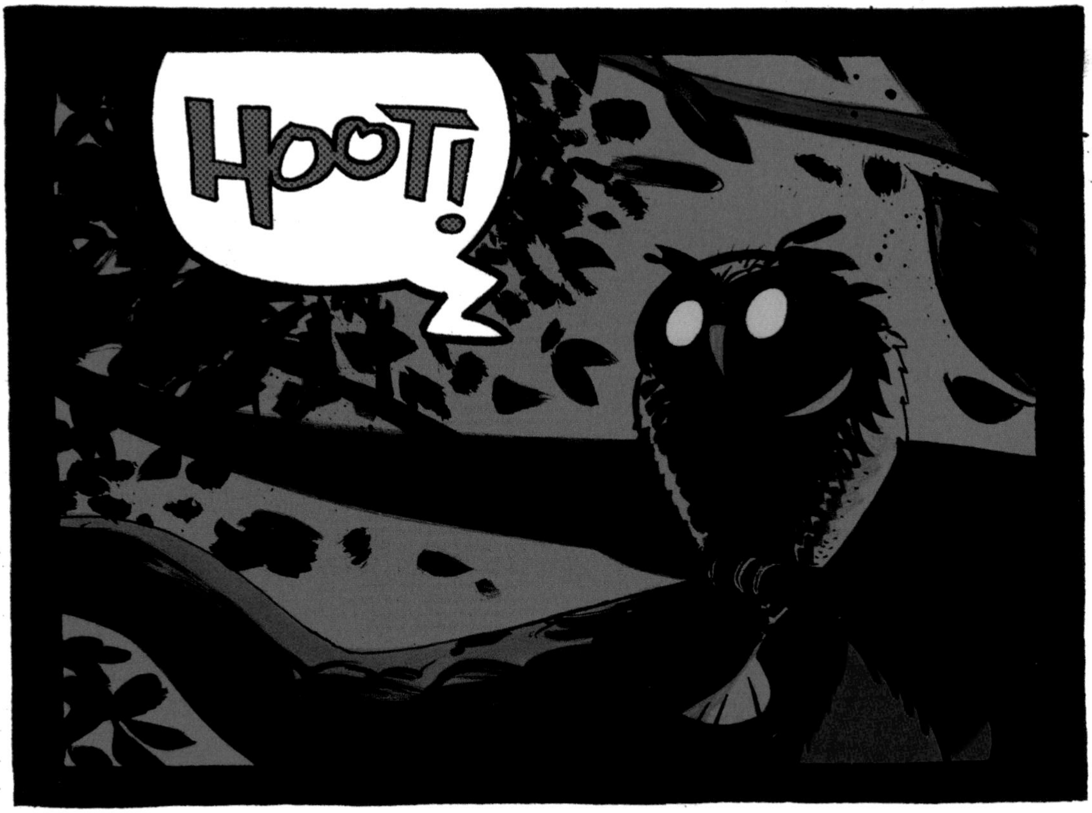
HOOT!

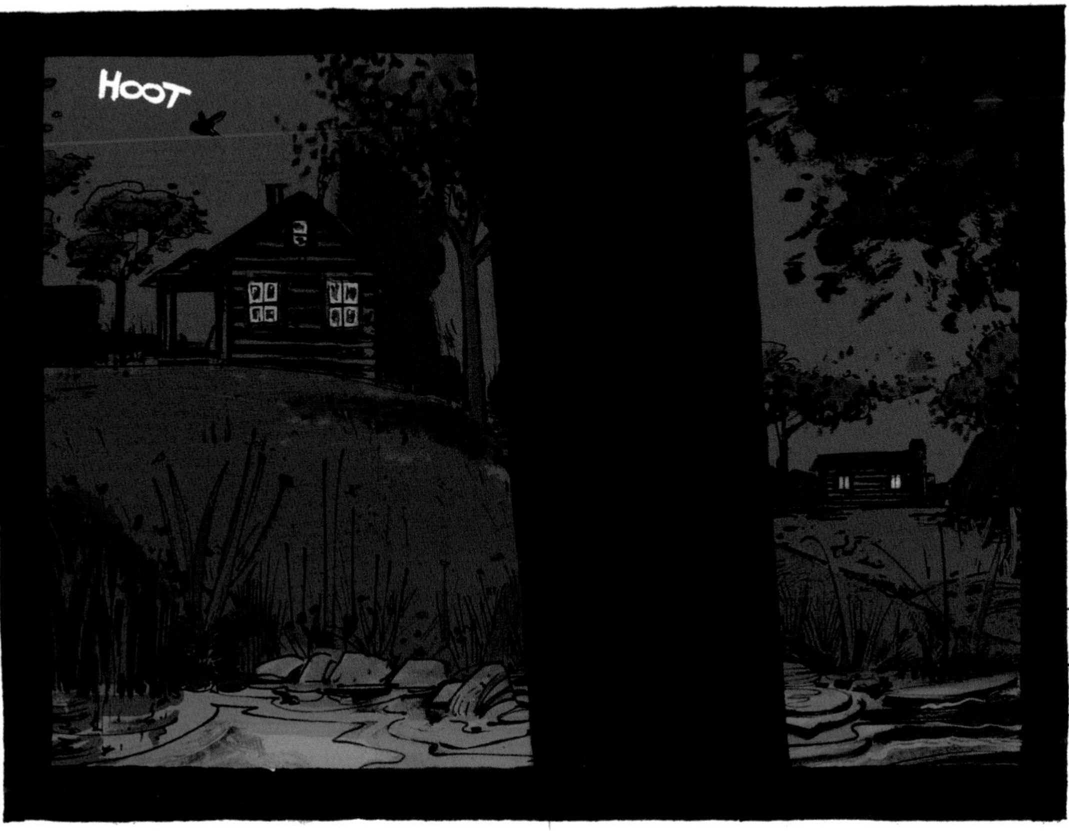
HOOT

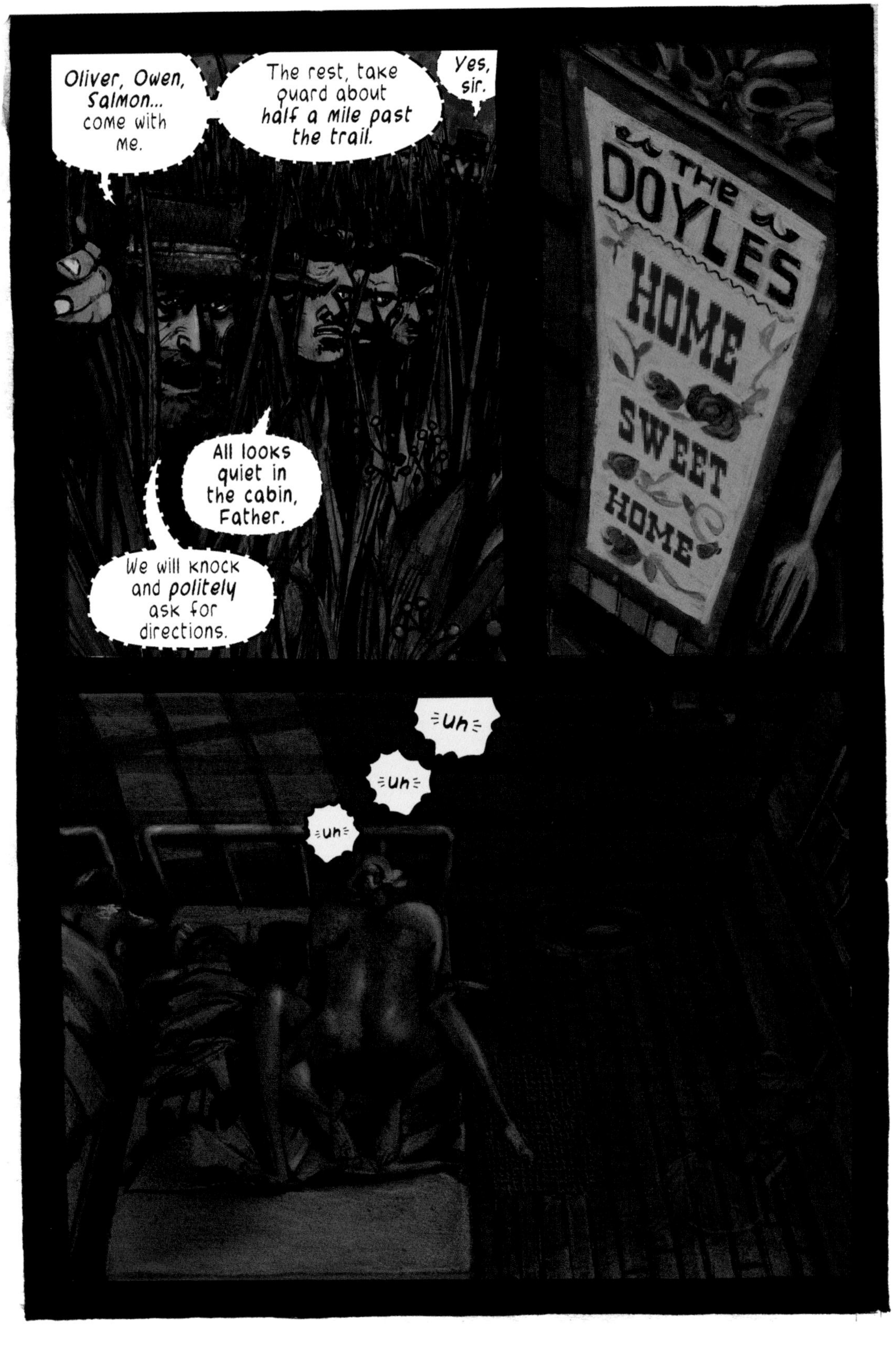
Oliver, Owen, Salmon... come with me.
The rest, take guard about half a mile past the trail.
Yes, sir.
All looks quiet in the cabin, Father.
We will knock and politely ask for directions.
THE DOYLES HOME SWEET HOME
uh
uh
uh

BARK
BARK
yiip!
Did you hear, father? The dogs!
Bucky? Rusty?!?
Boys-- back to sleep, will ya?
"It's just the wind."

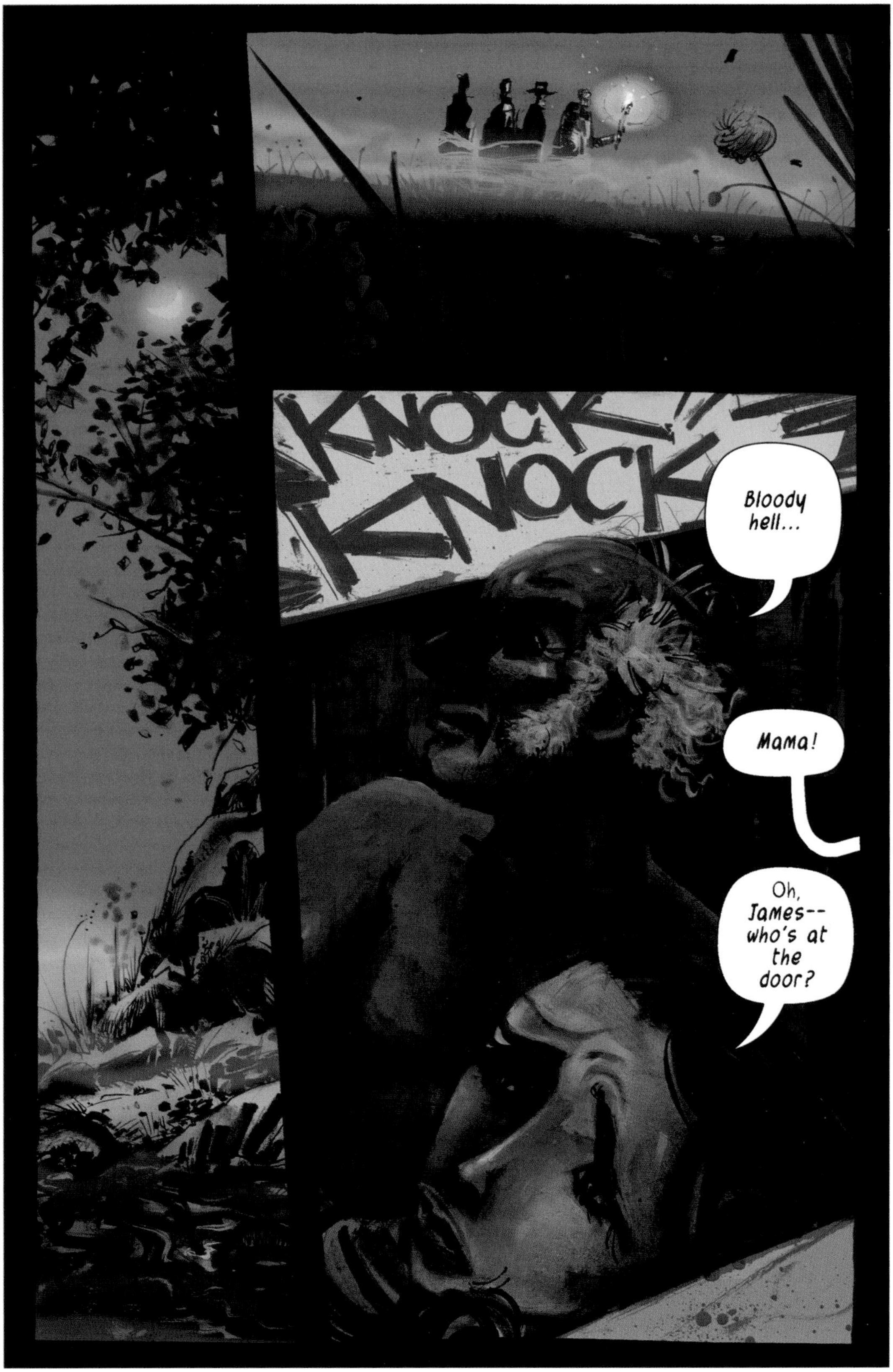
KNOCK
KNOCK
Bloody hell...
Mama!
Oh, James-- who's at the door?

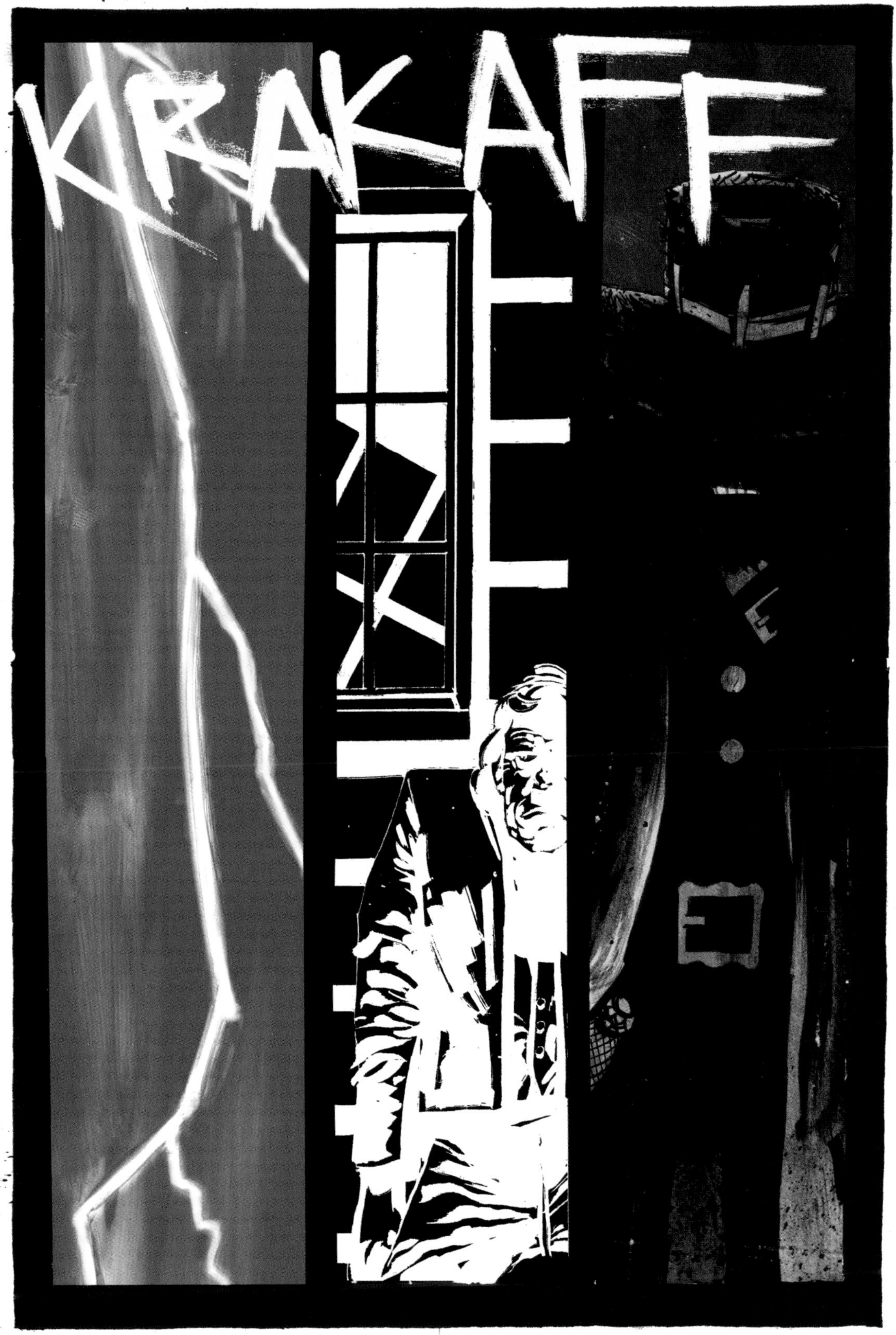
KRAKAFF

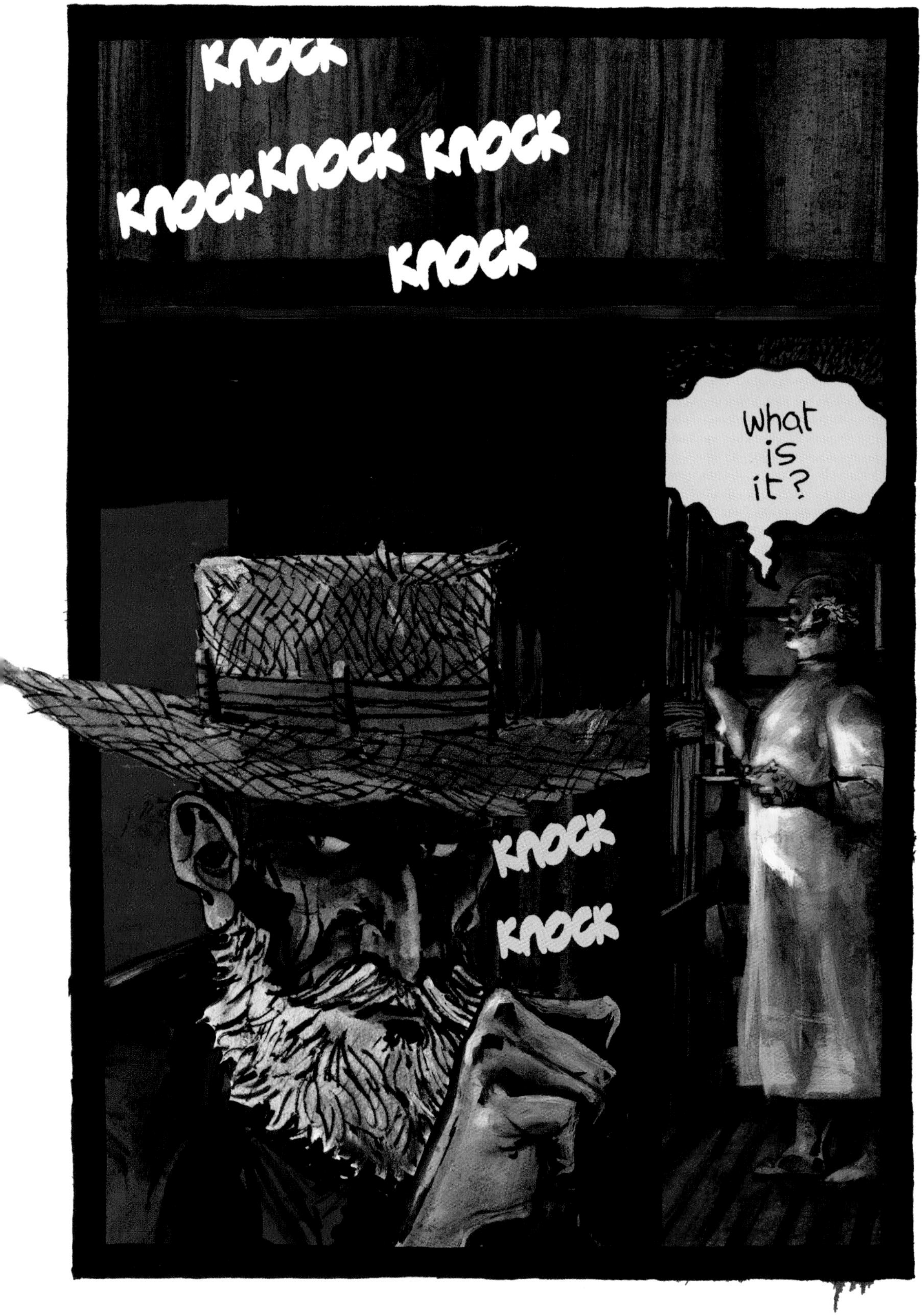
knock
knock knock knock
knock
what is it?
knock
knock

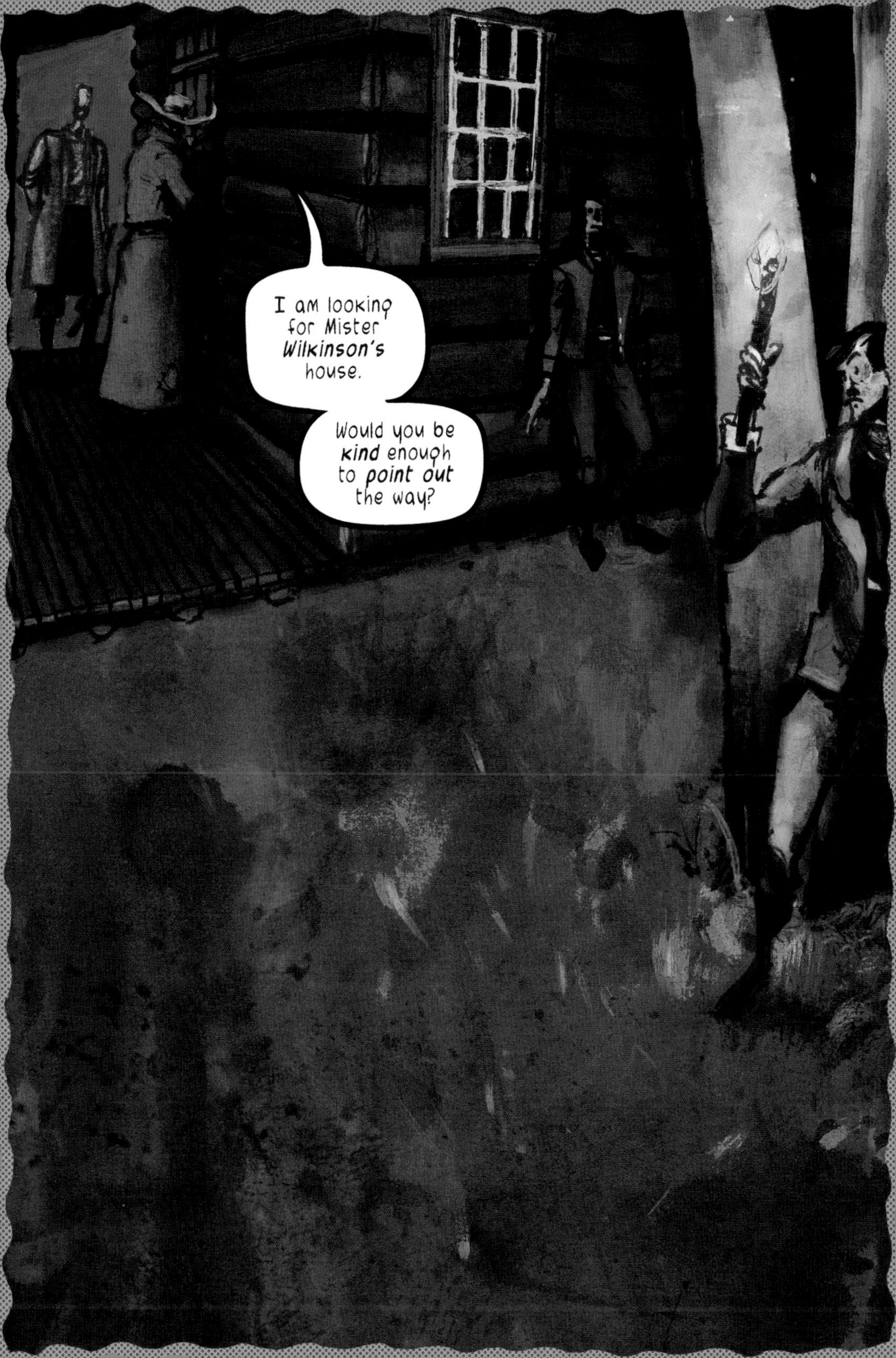
I am looking for Mister Wilkinson's house.
Would you be kind enough to point out the way?

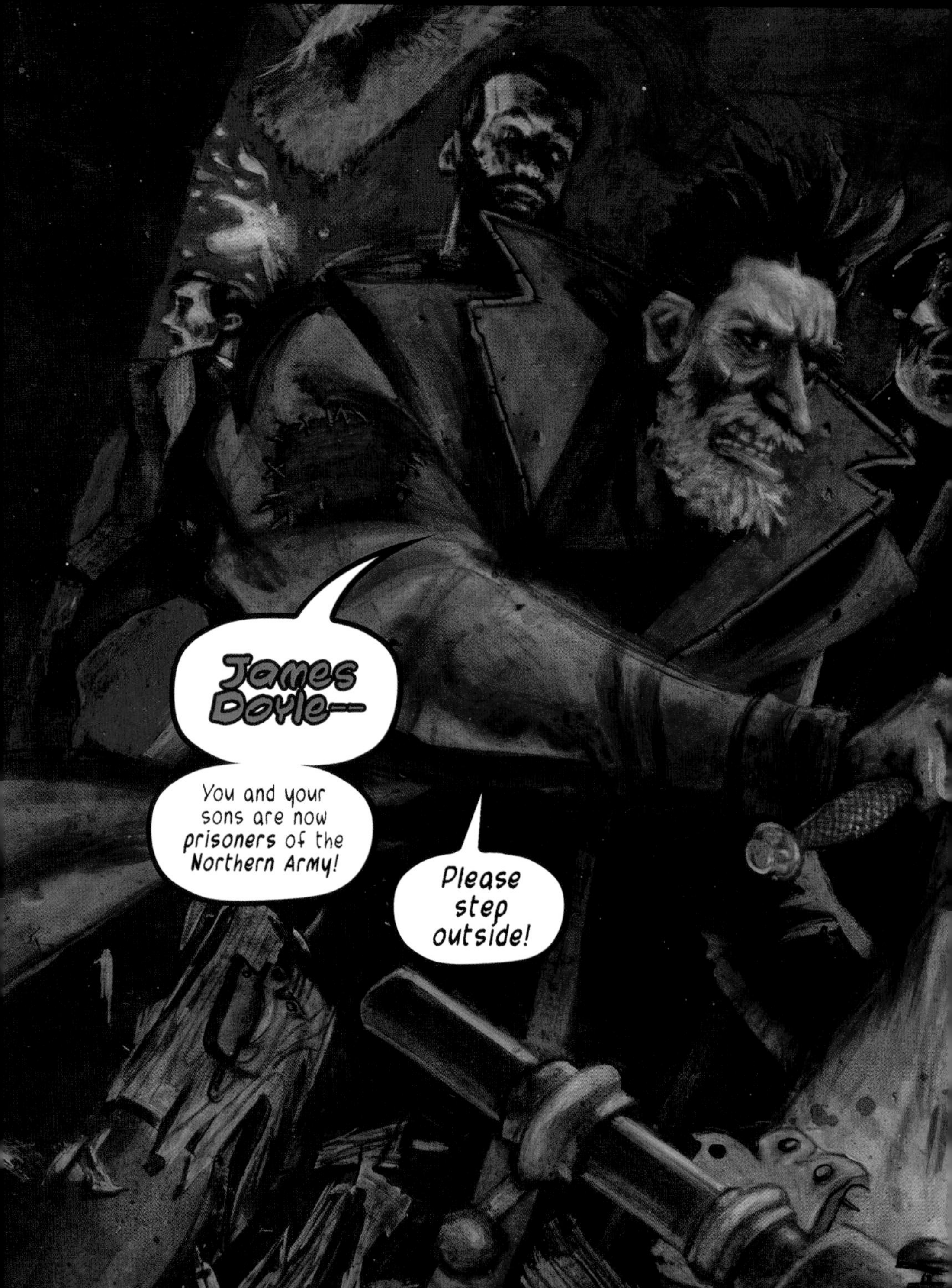
James Doyle--
You and your sons are now prisoners of the Northern Army!
Please step outside!

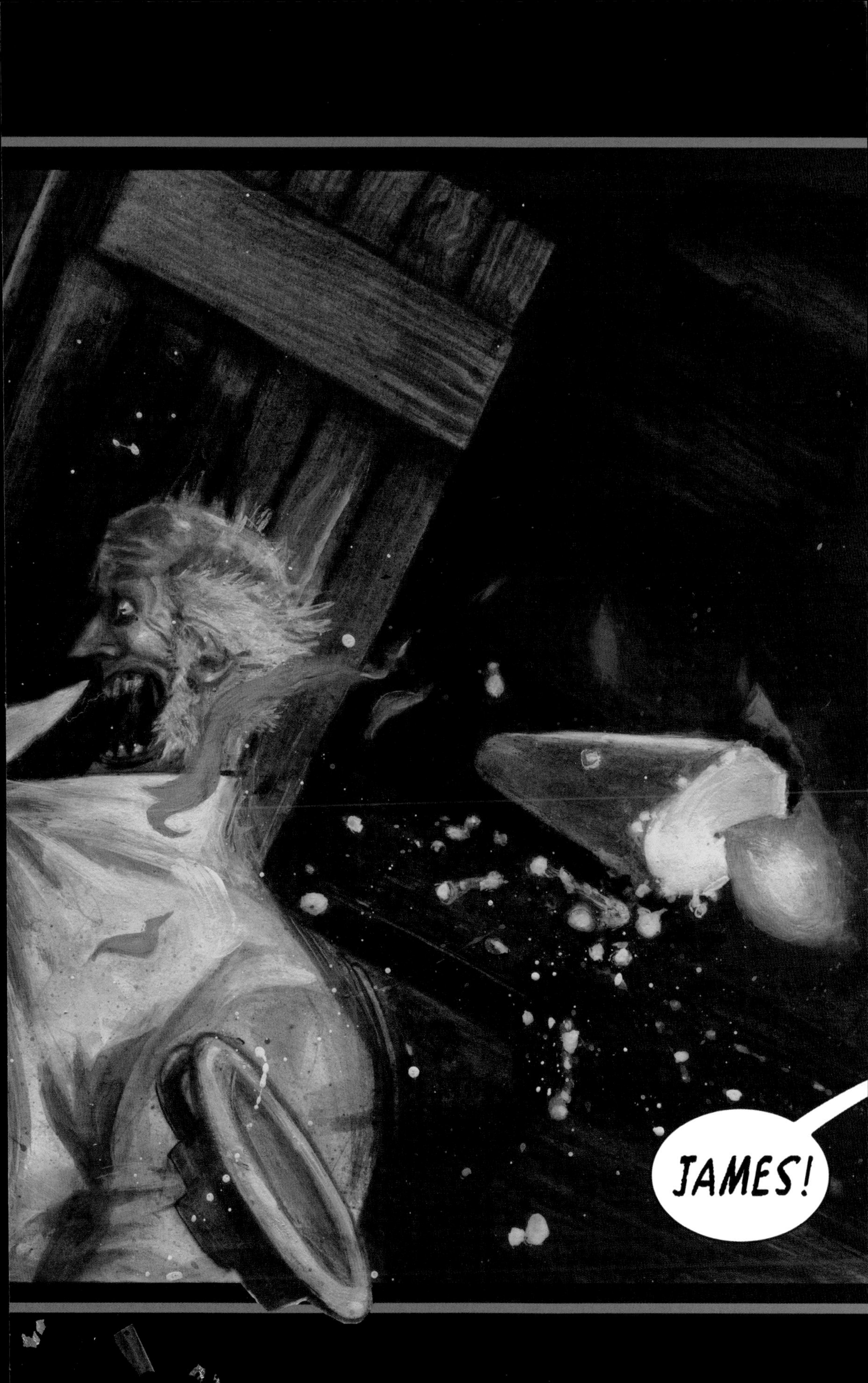
JAMES!

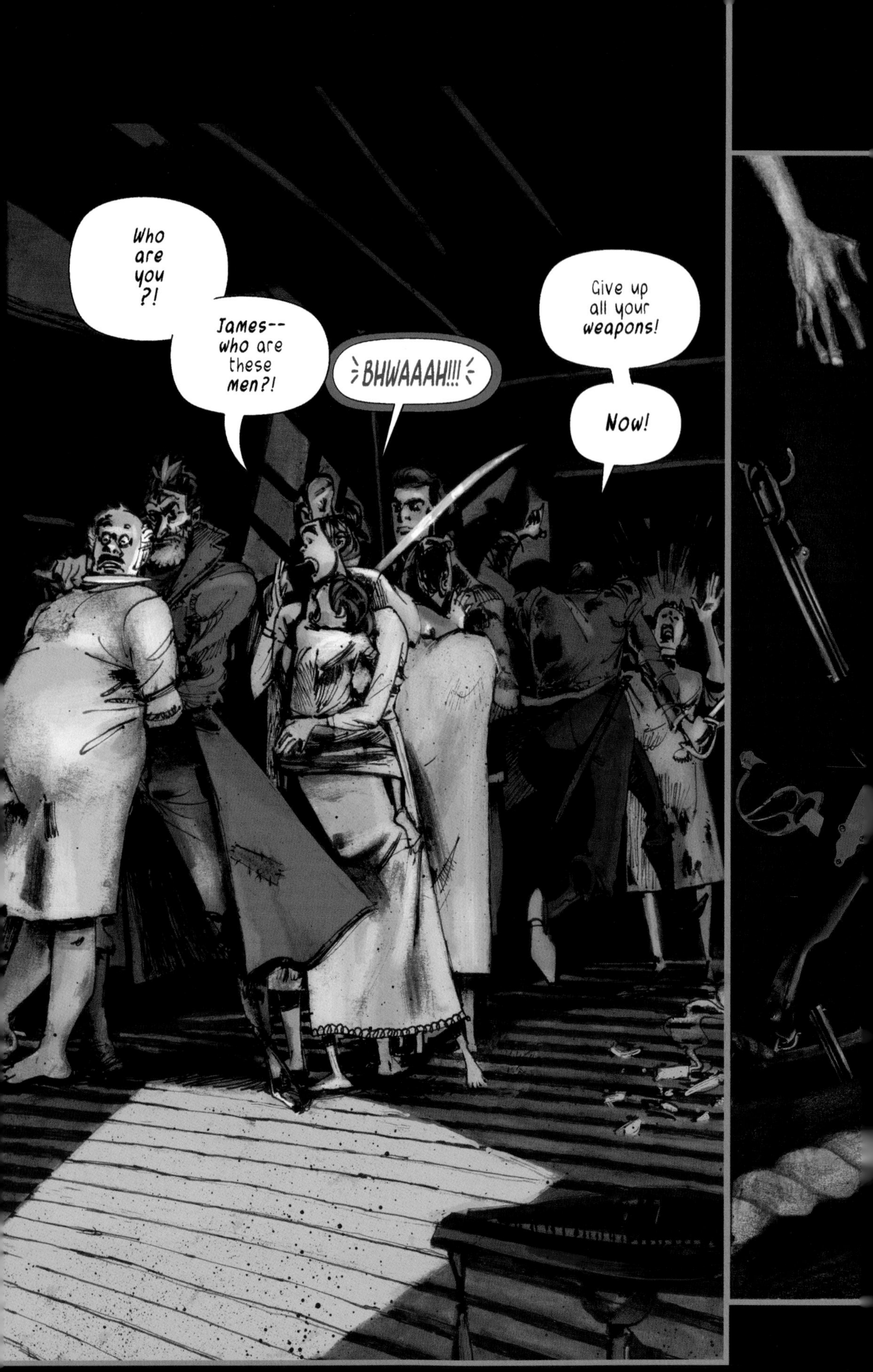
Who are you ?!
James-- who are these men?!
BHWAAAH!!!
Give up all your weapons!
Now!

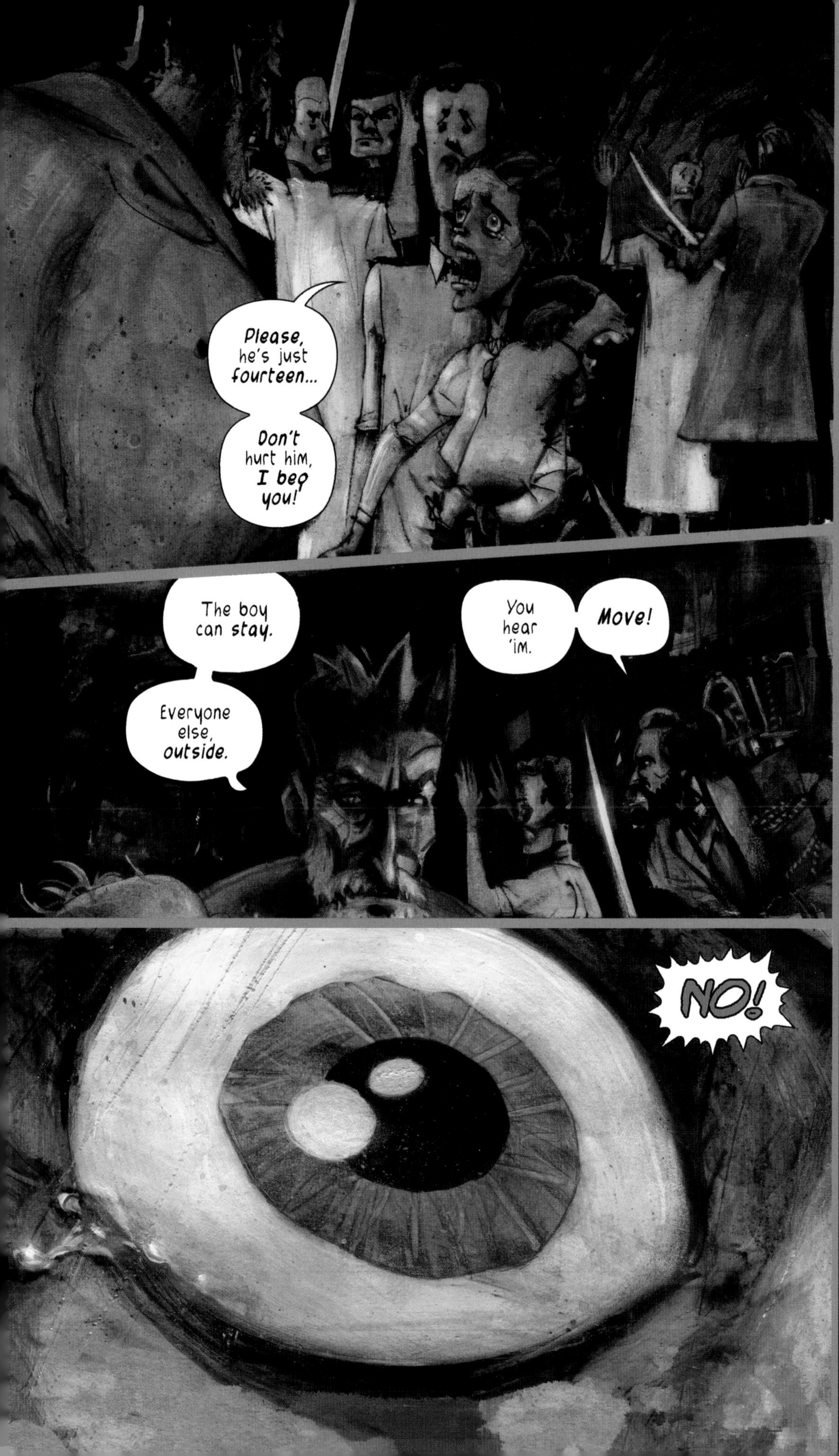

Please, he's just fourteen...
Don't hurt him, I beg you!
The boy can stay.
Everyone else, outside.
You hear 'im.
Move!
NO!

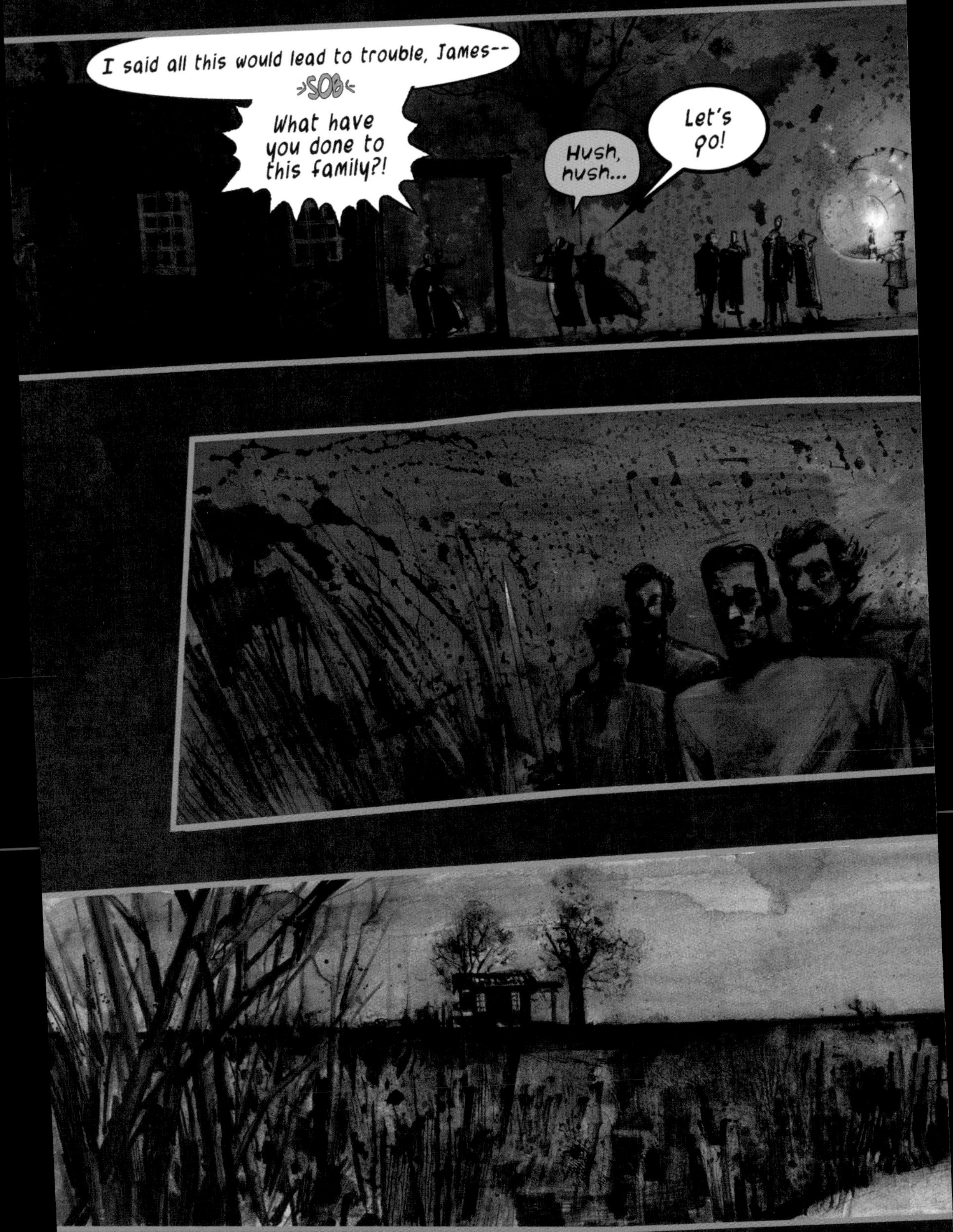
I said all this would lead to trouble, James--
SOB
What have you done to this family?!
Hush, hush...
Let's go!

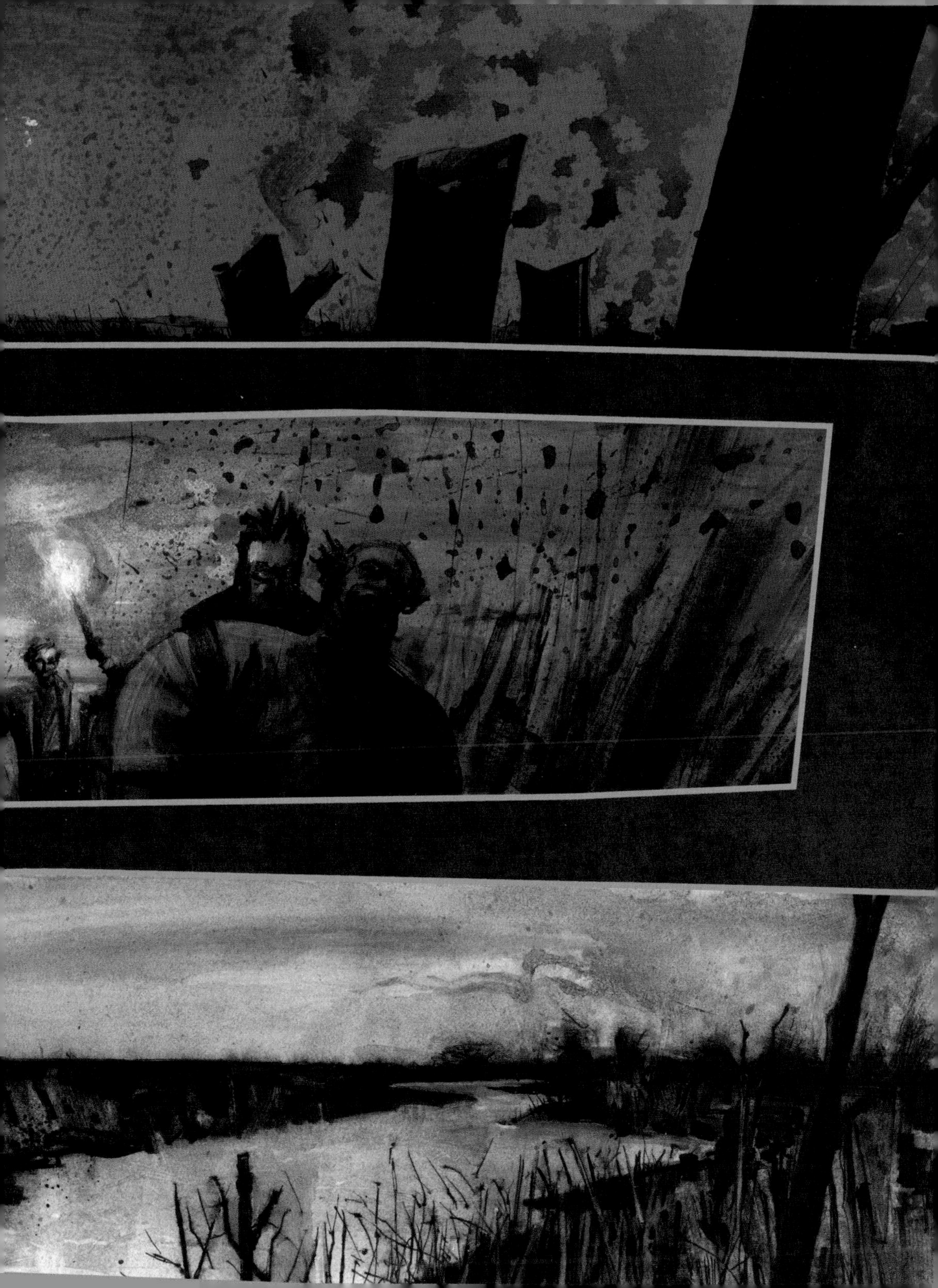

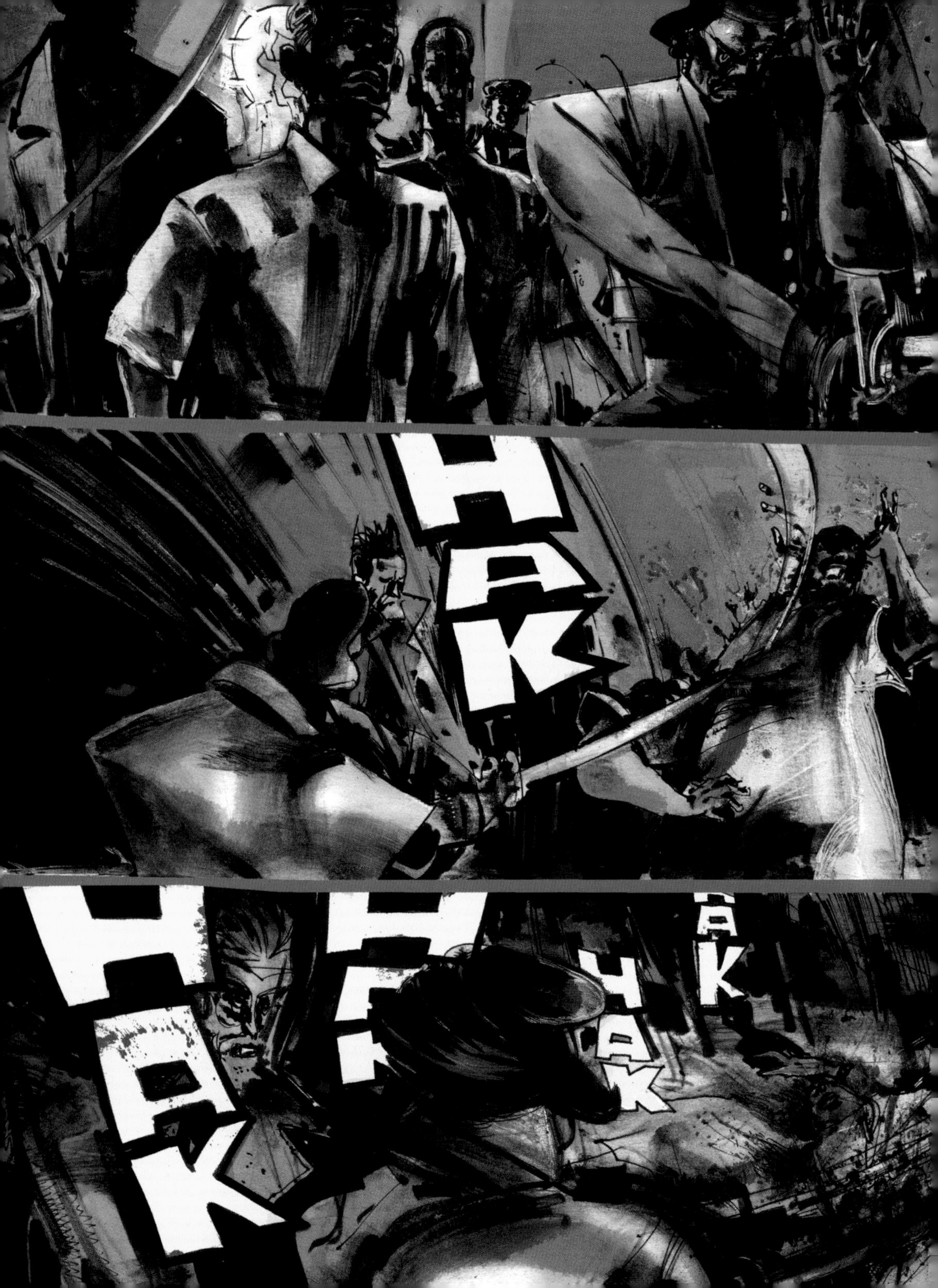
HAK
HAK
HAK
AK
HAK

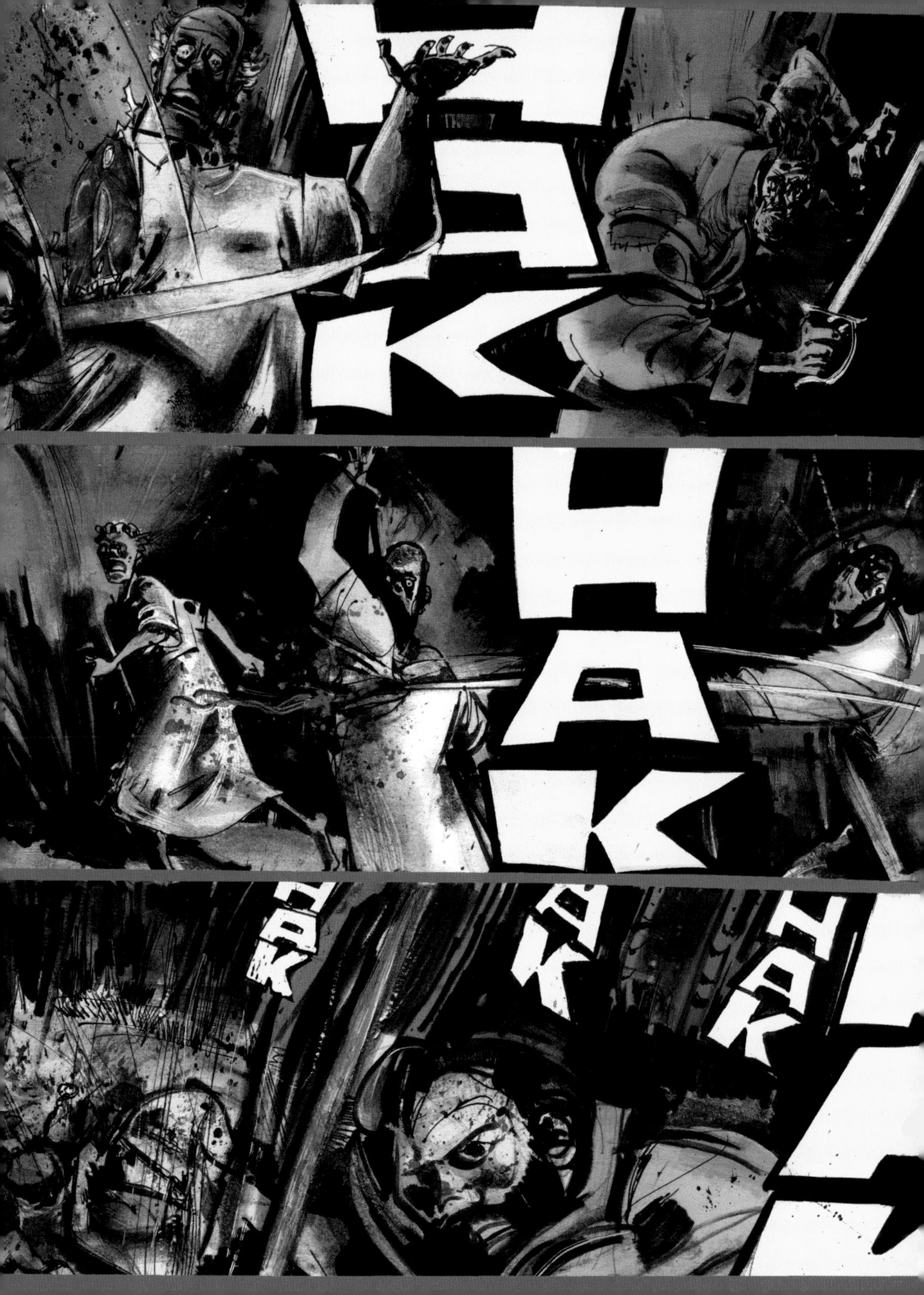

HAK
HAK
HAK
HAK
HAK

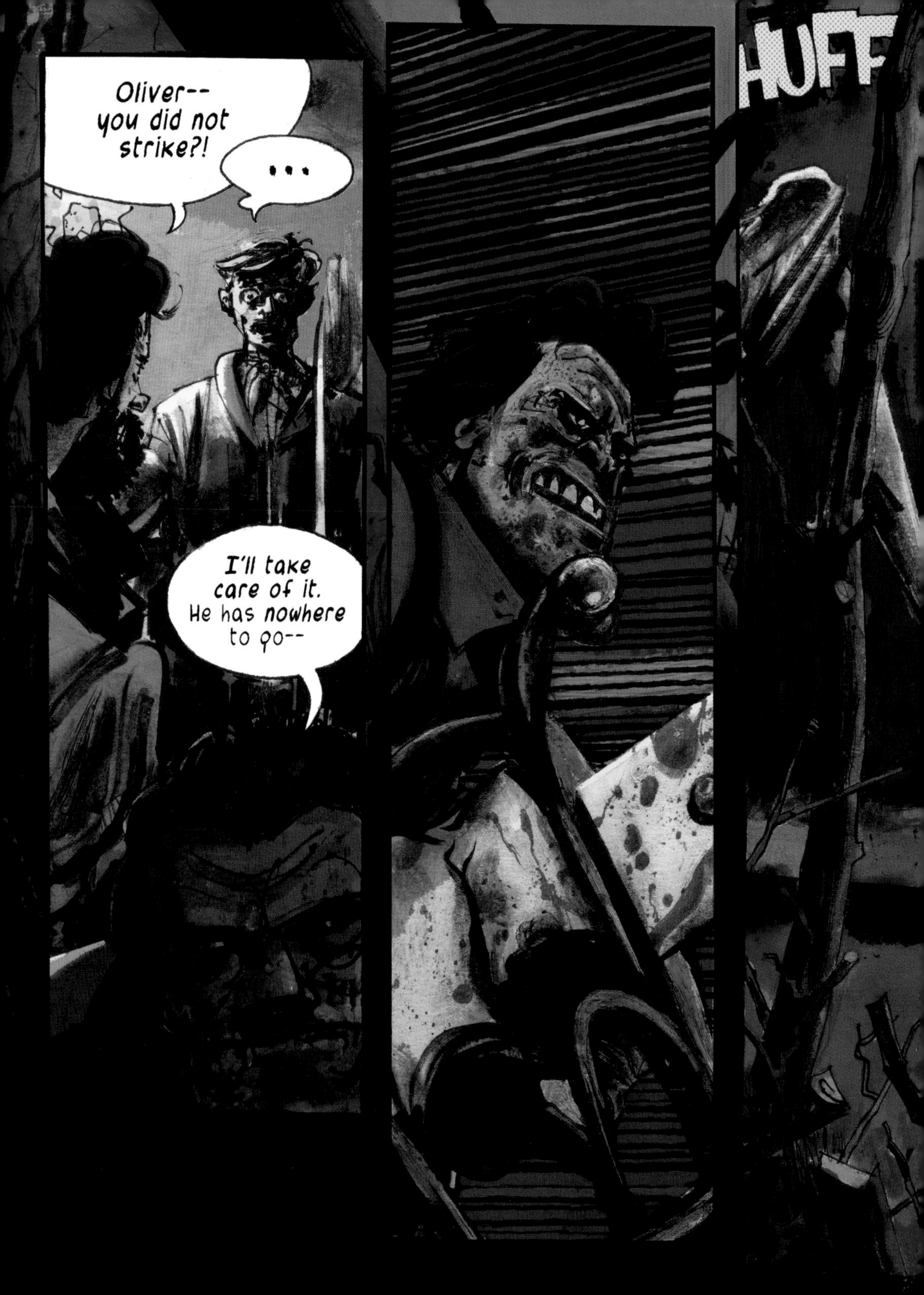
Oliver-- you did not strike?!
...
I'll take care of it. He has *nowhere* to go--
HUFF

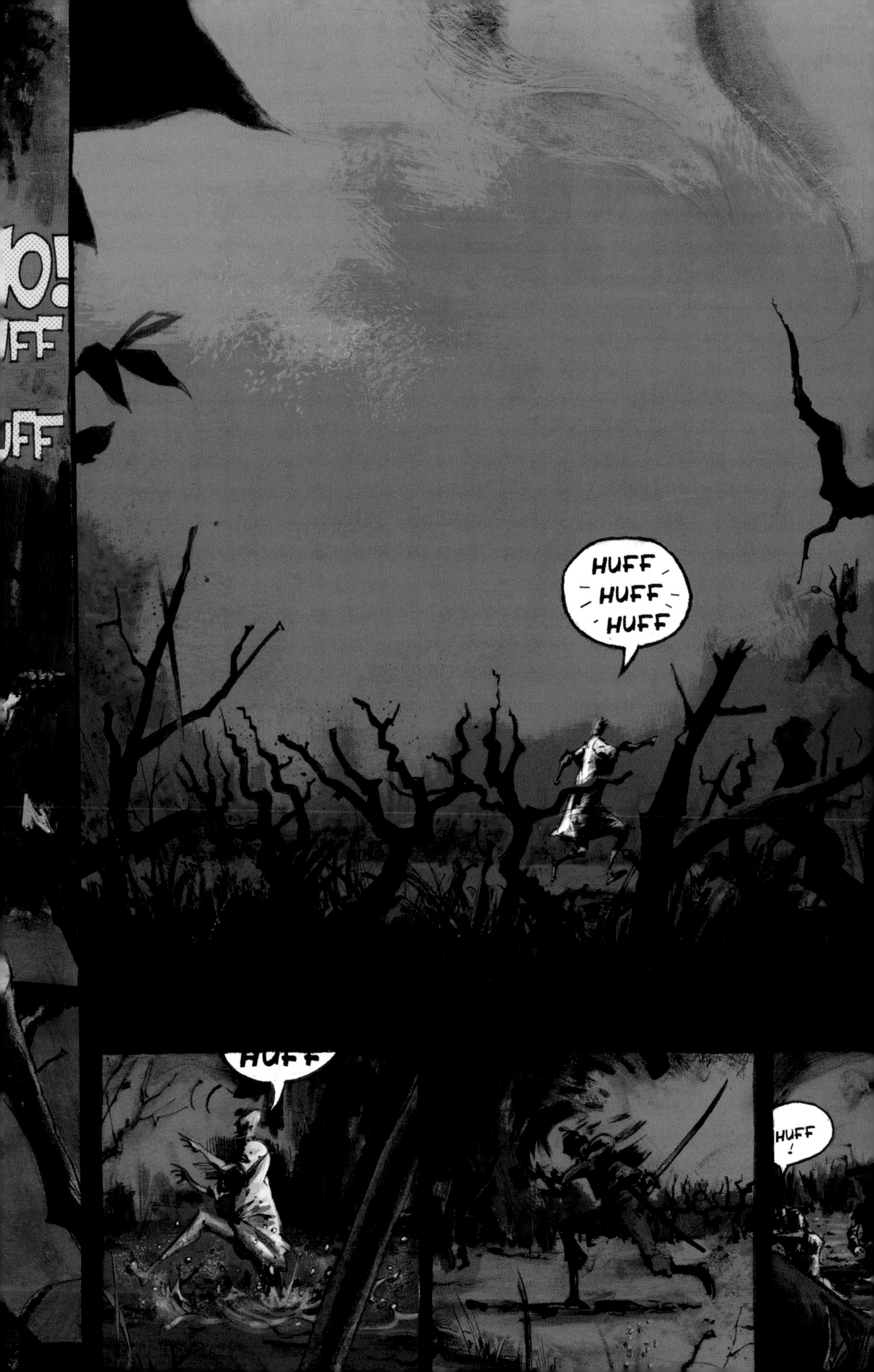
HUFF HUFF HUFF
HUFF
HUFF !

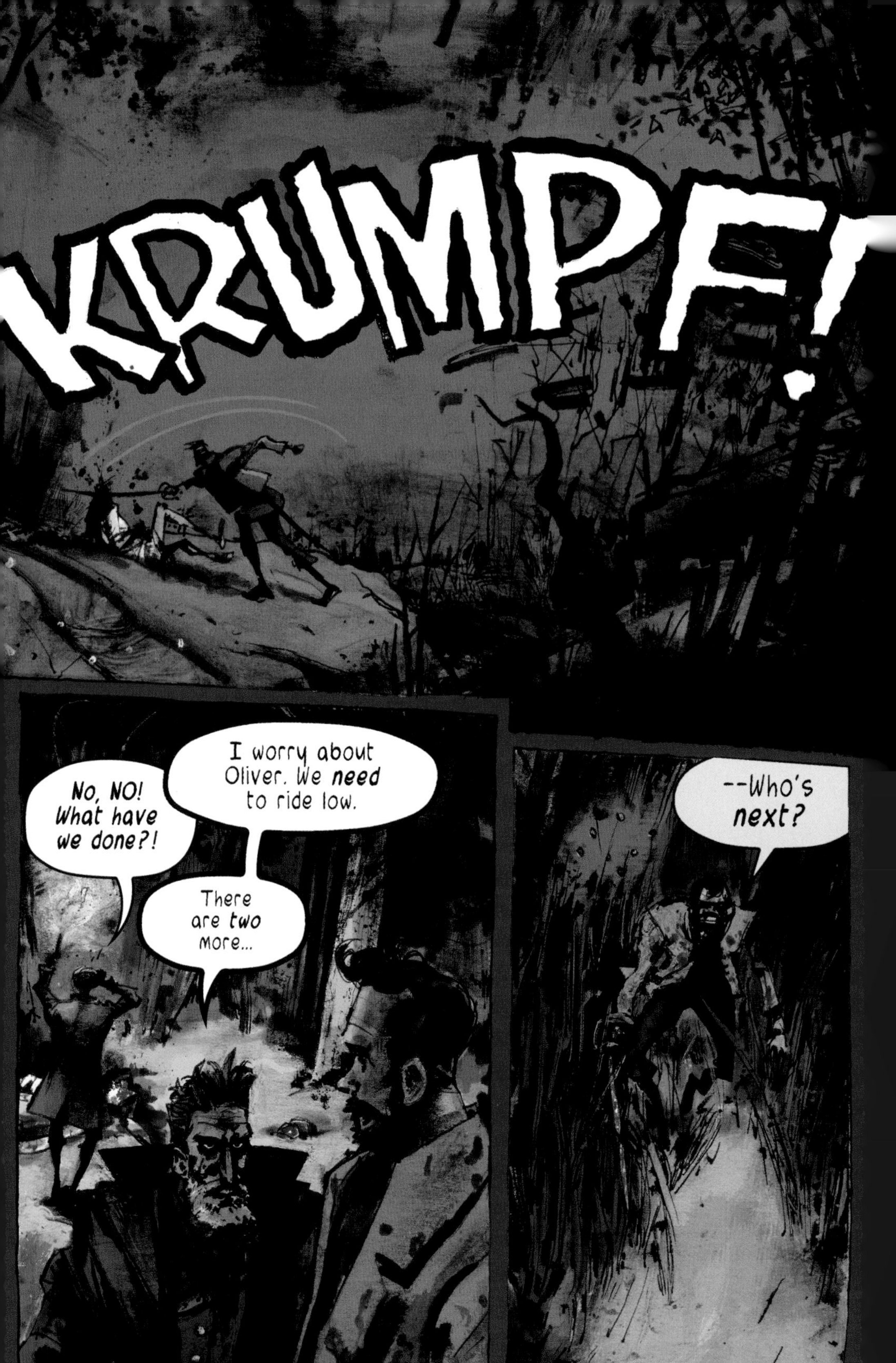
KRUMPF!
No, NO! What have we done?!
I worry about Oliver. We need to ride low.
There are two more...
--Who's next?

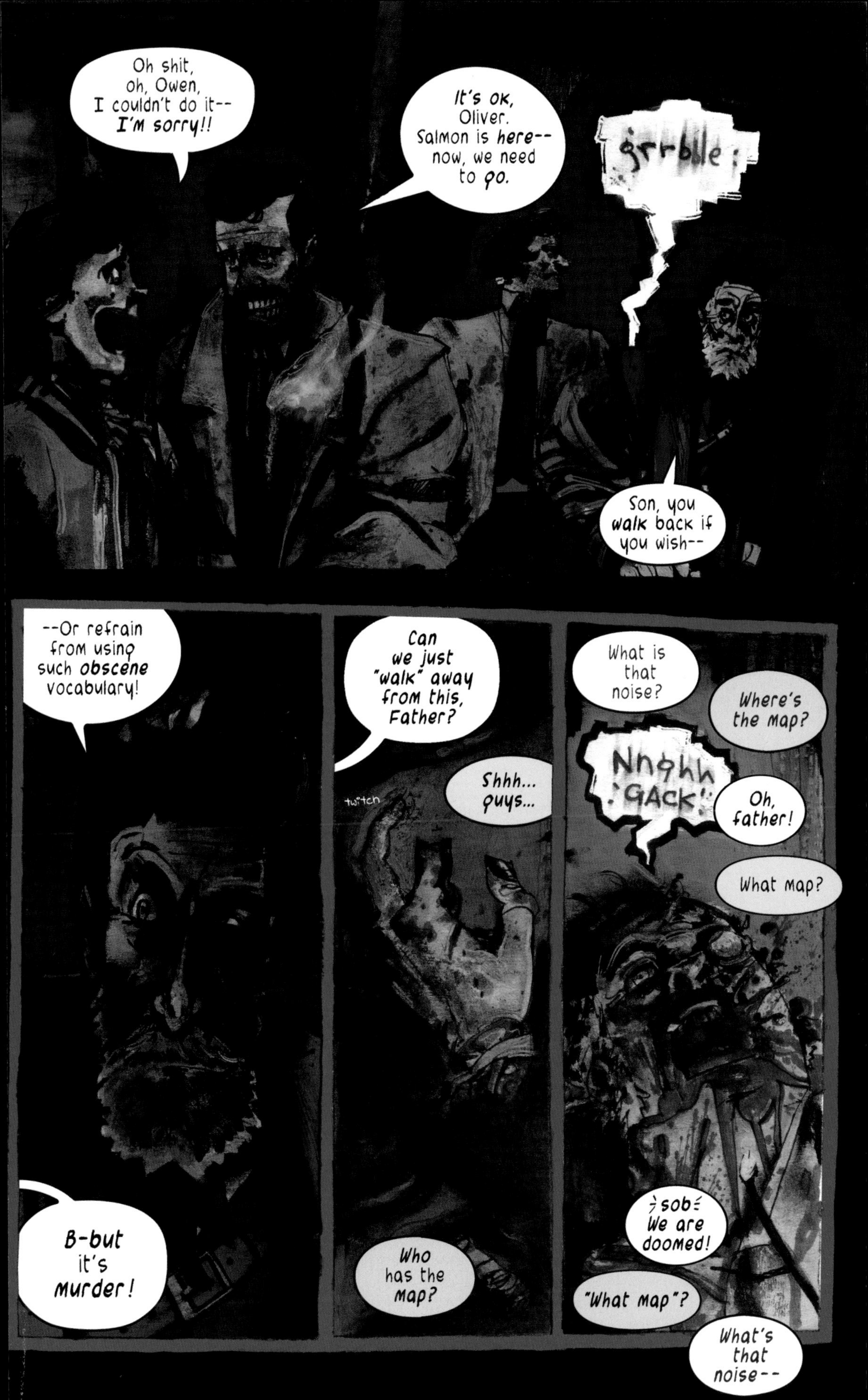
Oh shit, oh, Owen, I couldn't do it-- I'M sorry!!
It's OK, Oliver. Salmon is here-- now, we need to go.
grrbble
Son, you walk back if you wish--
--Or refrain from using such obscene vocabulary!
B-but it's murder!
Can we just "walk" away from this, Father?
twitch
Shhh... guys...
Who has the map?
What is that noise?
Where's the map?
Nnghh GACK!
Oh, father!
What map?
sob We are doomed!
"What map"?
What's that noise--

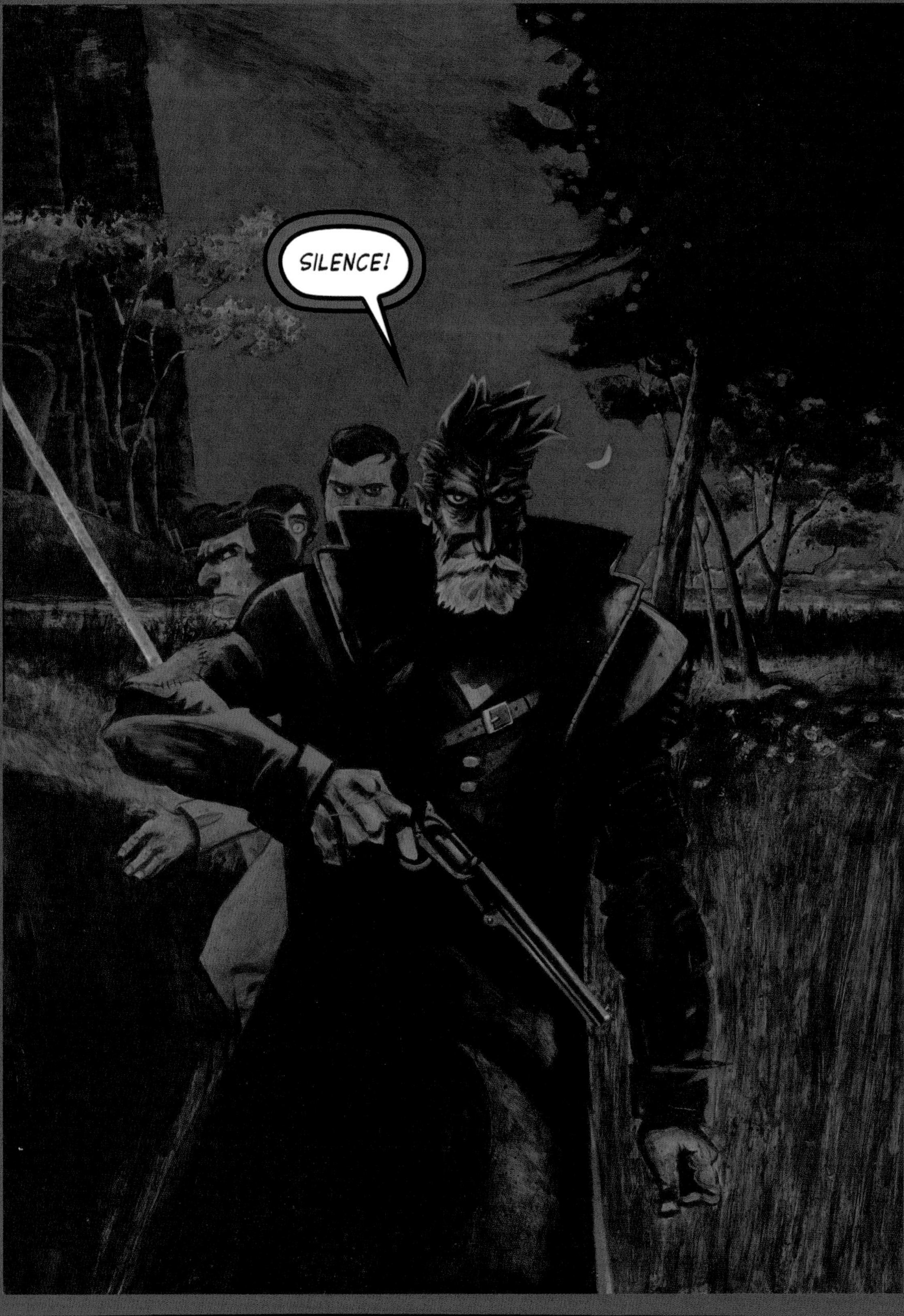
SILENCE!

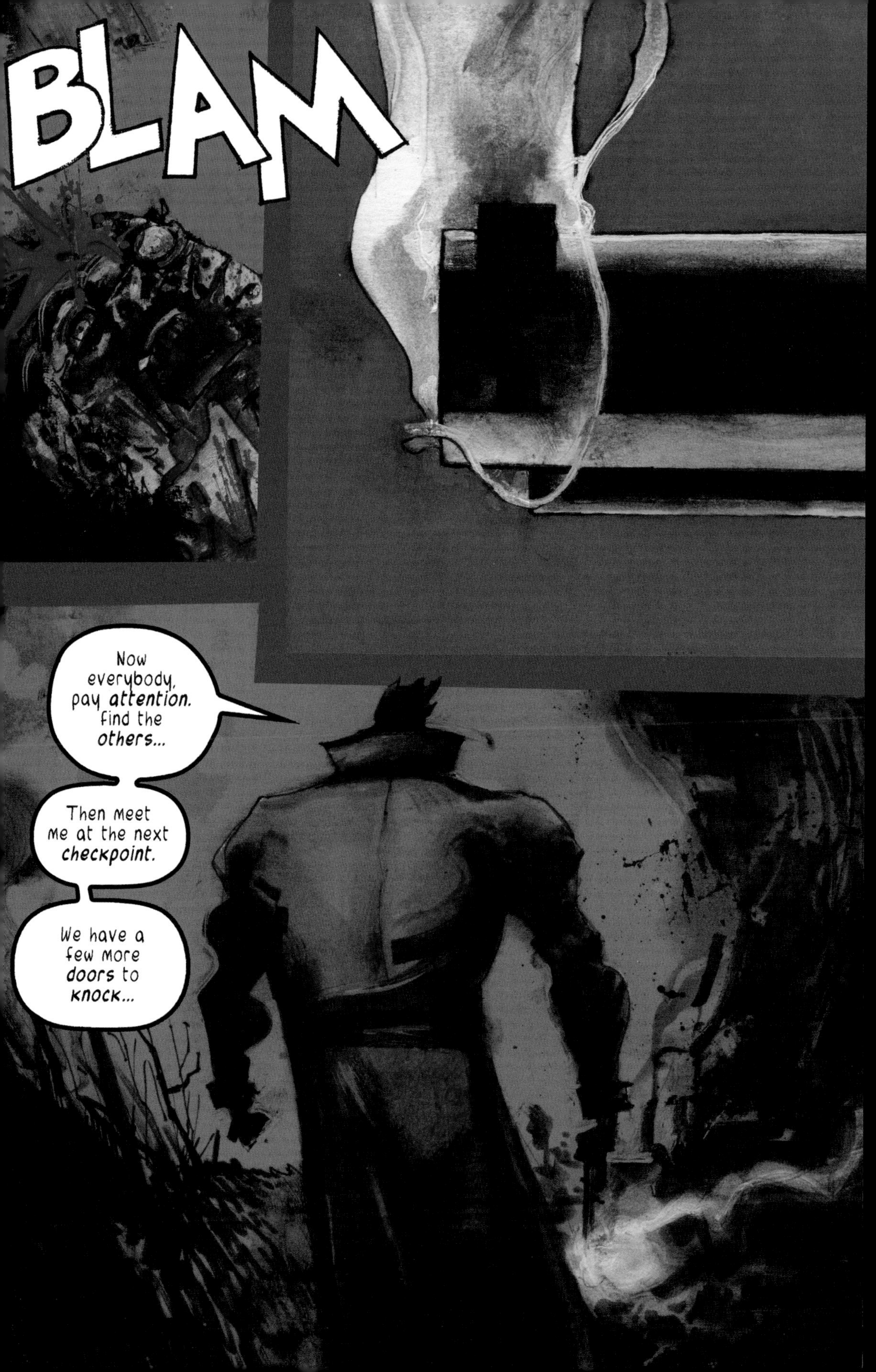
BLAM
Now everybody, pay attention. Find the others...
Then meet me at the next checkpoint.
We have a few more doors to knock...

Knock Knock

We need directions to *Dutch Henry's...*

Well, uh... turn *left* about a mile fr--

Who's there?

I can barely hear you...

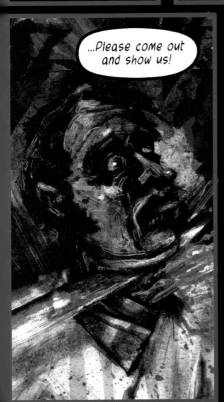

...Please come out and show us!

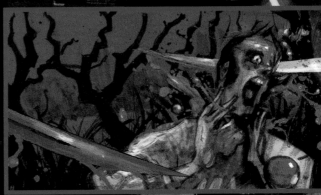

Knock

Knock

DUTCH HENRY'S TAVERN

Where is Henry Sherman!?

D-Dutch Henry is not here, stranger!

This-is-- my cabin! These are my guests.

Bah! What is *troubling* you, old man !?!

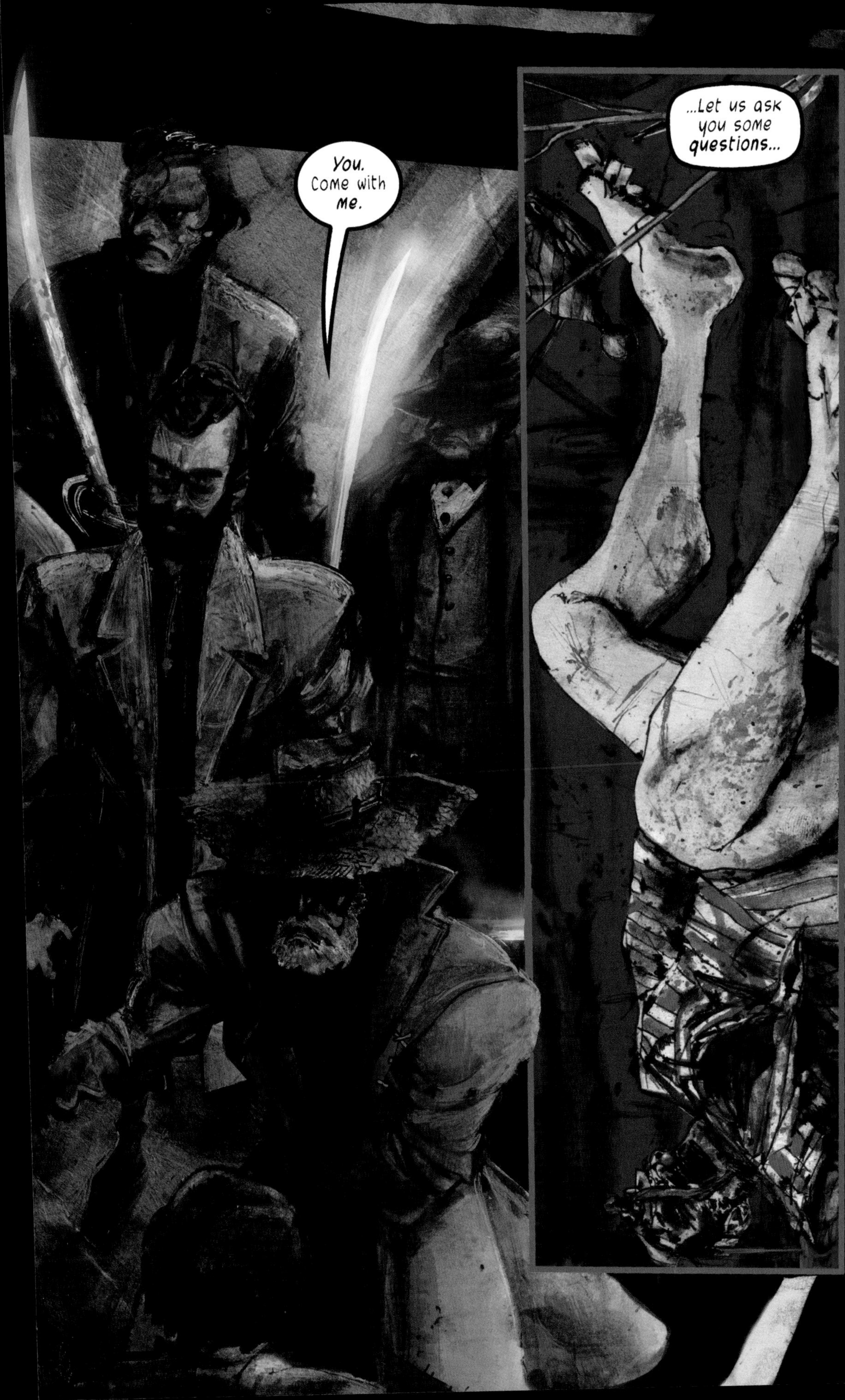
You. Come with me.
...Let us ask you some questions...

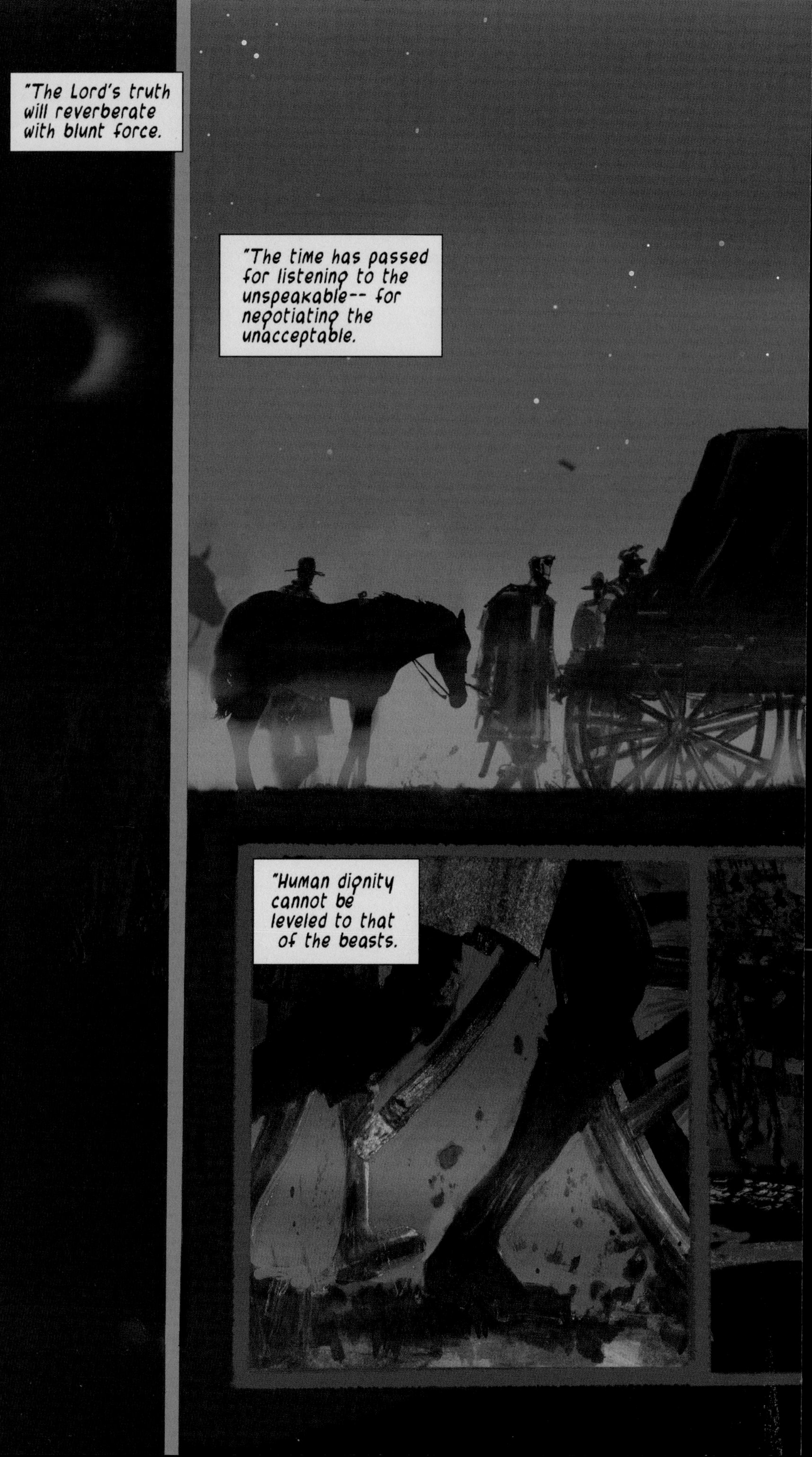
"The Lord's truth will reverberate with blunt force.
"The time has passed for listening to the unspeakable-- for negotiating the unacceptable.
"Human dignity cannot be leveled to that of the beasts.

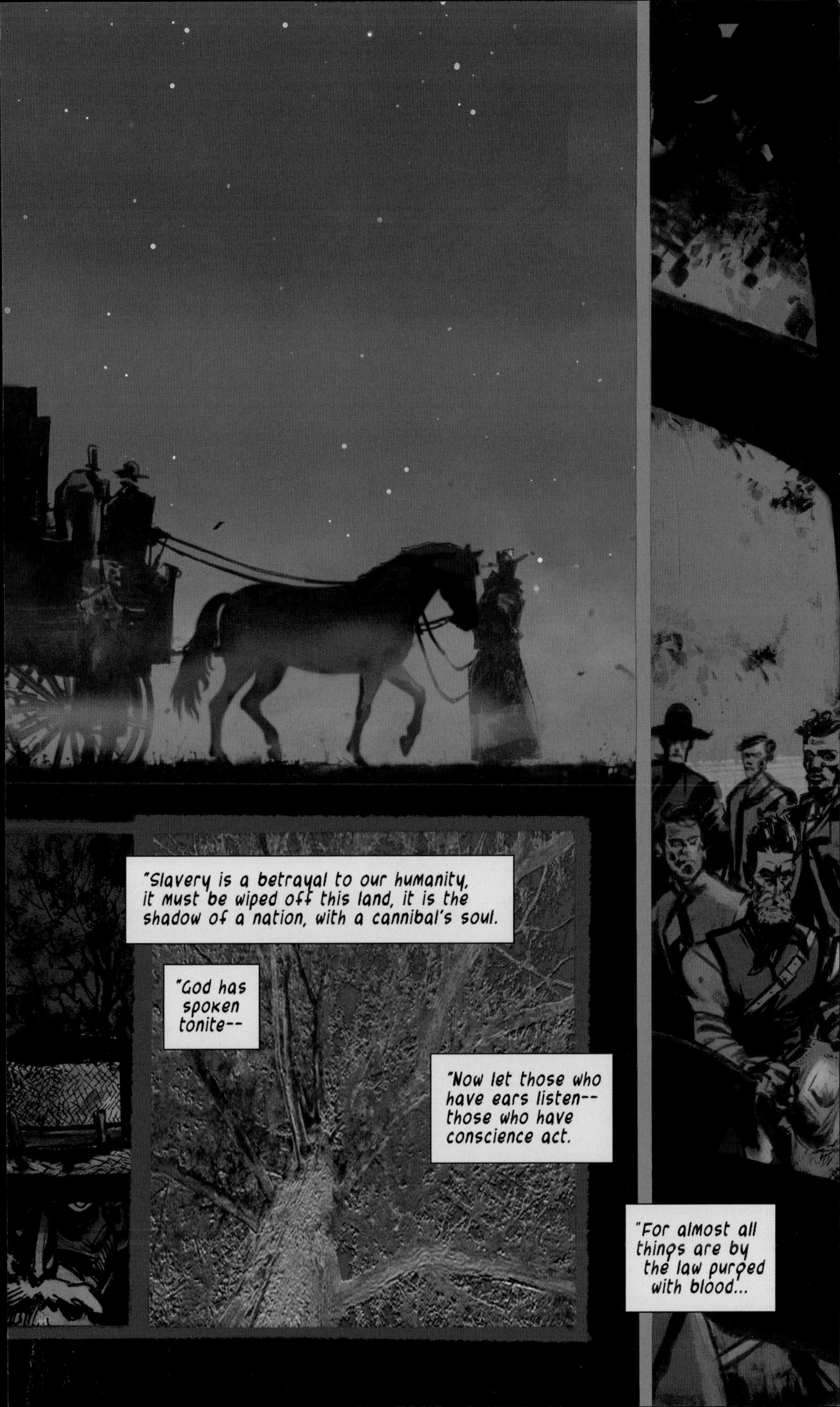
"Slavery is a betrayal to our humanity, it must be wiped off this land, it is the shadow of a nation, with a cannibal's soul.
"God has spoken tonite--
"Now let those who have ears listen--those who have conscience act.
"For almost all things are by the law purged with blood...

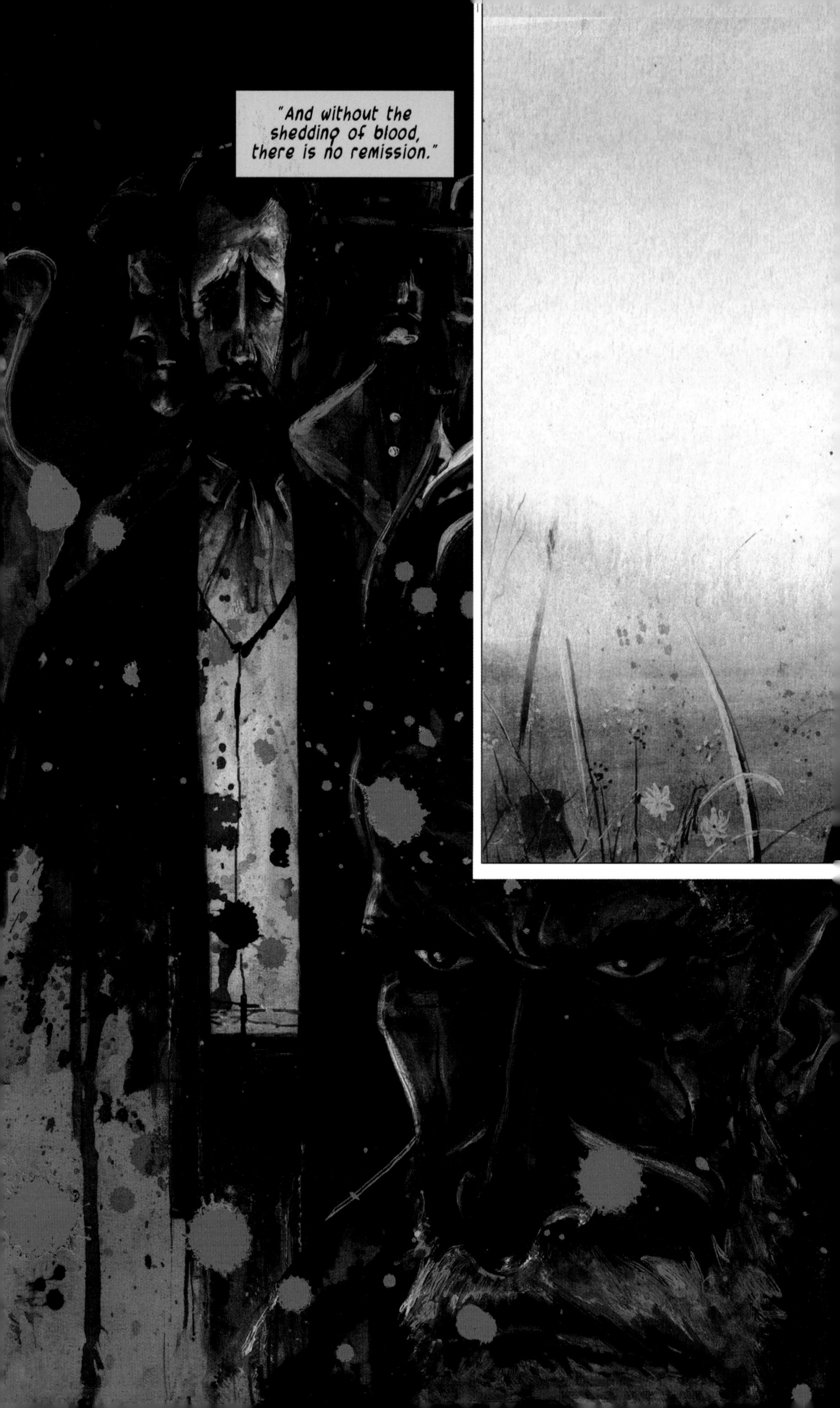
"And without the shedding of blood, there is no remission."

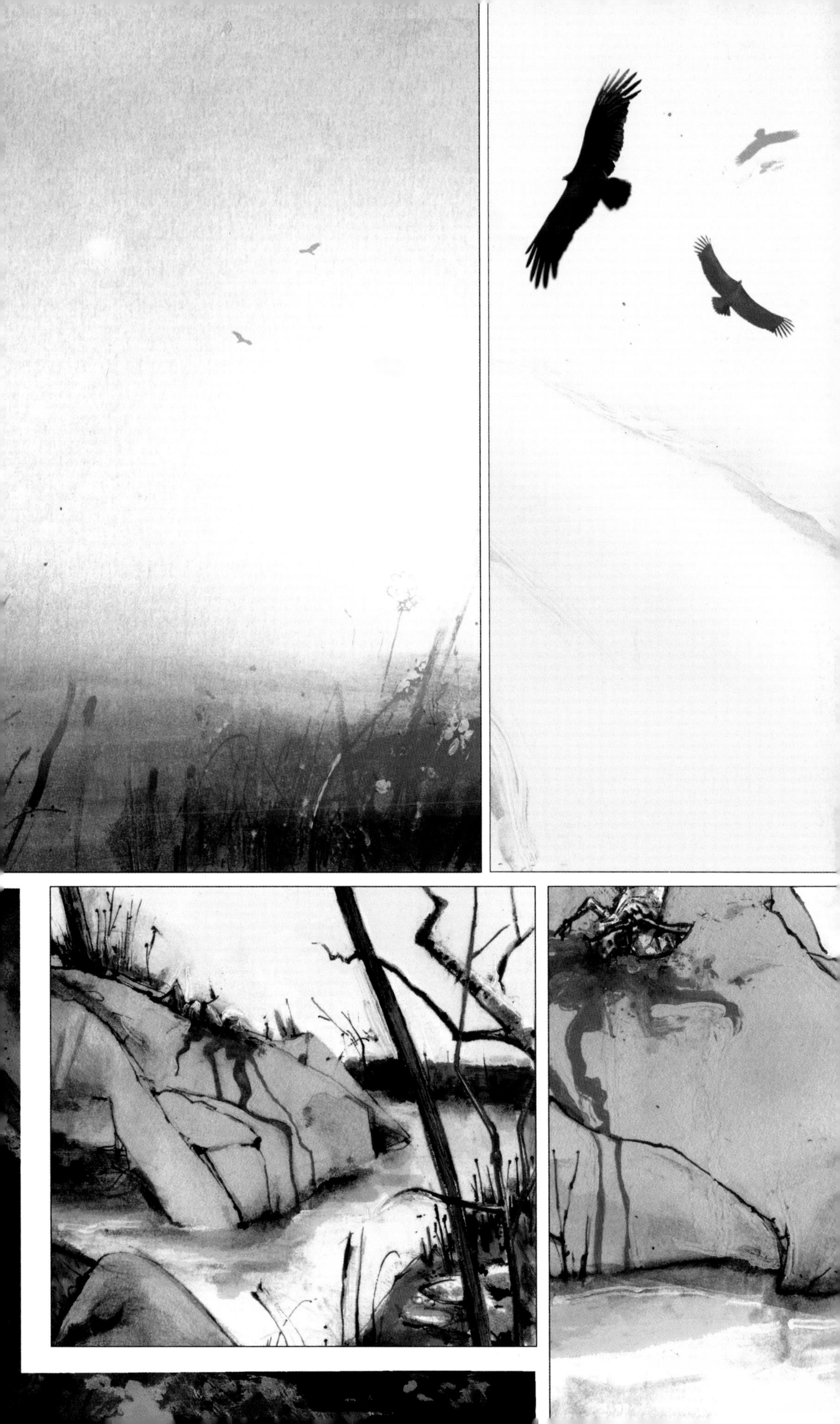

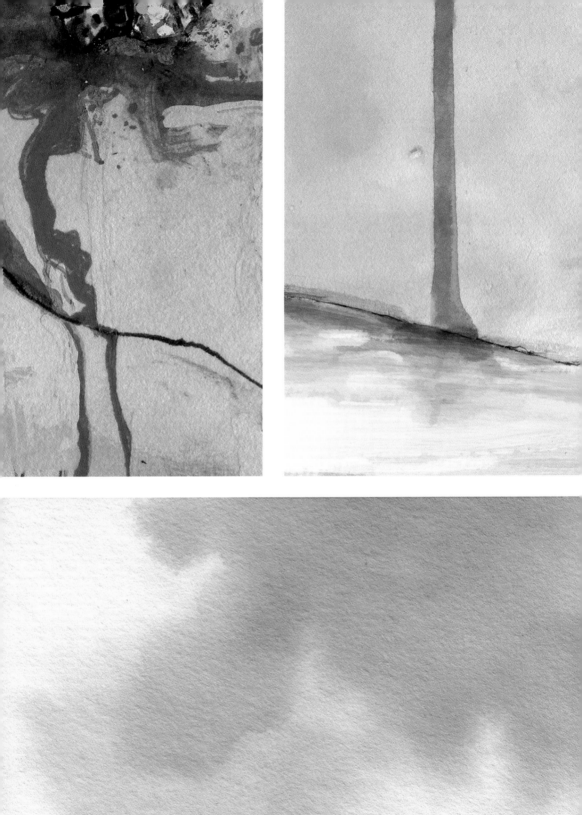

2

EIGHT MEN BRUTALLY MURDERED BY THE ABOLITIONISTS!

The following letter was received by a messenger from Franklin county, K.T., this morning, which was written by the Commissioner of Franklin county. Eight men were known to be killed -- three by the name of Doyle, three by the name of Sherman, a Mr. Whiteman and a Mr. Wilkerson. The messenger who brought the information to Franklin states that he had seen the party who were murdered; they were cut to pieces and horribly mangled. For every southern man thus butchered, a decade of these poltroons should bite the dust.

The gentlemen in the vicinity of these outrages were of the opinion that Gov. Shannon was at the Swawnee Mission, and the letter containing the intelligence was sent by the sons of Mr. Wm. Muir of this county. They arrived at the residence of their father early this morning. The letter has been forwarded to Gov. Shannon. Franklin Co., K. T., Sunday May 25, '56. To the Hon. Gov. of Kansas Territory, of the Hon. Daniel Woodson, Secretary of the Territory:

Gentlemen -- I will inform your Honors that there is a mob of the Yankees in this part of the Territory, committing dreadful outrages of the most savage character.

An express arrived this morning at my place of residence, from Pottawatomie Creek, with information that an organized body of Abolitionists, at a very late hour last night, attacked the houses of the pro-slavery men and tore them from their families and murdered them in cold blood in a most savage manner.

The informer states that he believes nearly all the pro-slavery men on Pottawatomie Creek were murdered last night. This is to inform you that it is now high time to send troops without delay. Send immediate relief until other arrangements can be made, and further information can be had.

Yours, in haste,
SAMUEL M. ROBERTSON
Co. Com. of Franklin Co.

The Glasgow Times.

Published every Thursday morning by
CLARK H. GREEN,
AT ONE DOLLAR PER ANNUM
INVARIABLY IN ADVANCE.

EAGLE FOUNDRY

ENTER THE BLADE

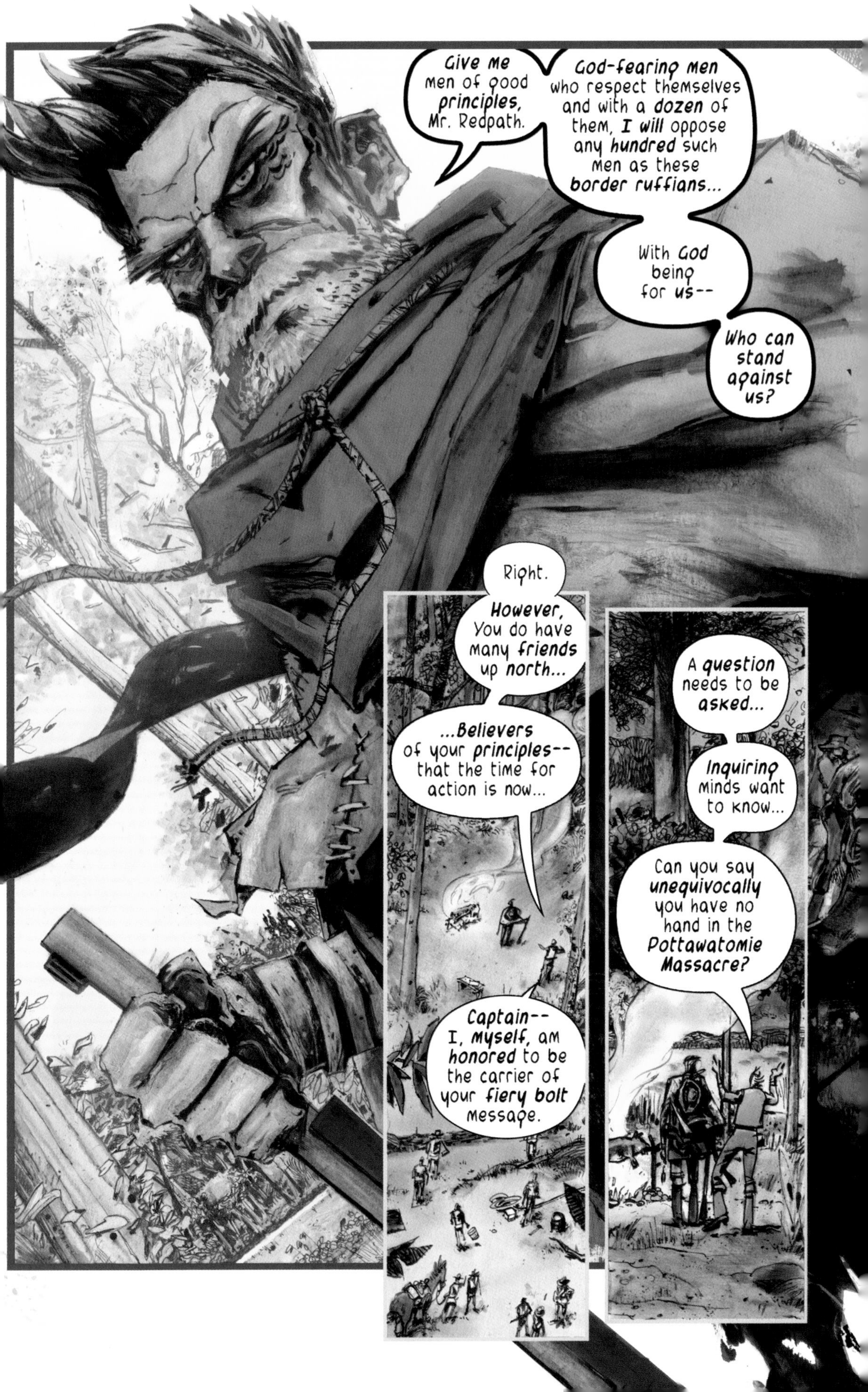

Give me men of good principles, Mr. Redpath.
God-fearing men who respect themselves and with a dozen of them, I will oppose any hundred such men as these border ruffians...
With God being for us--
Who can stand against us?
Right.
However, you do have many friends up north...
...Believers of your principles--that the time for action is now...
Captain--I, myself, am honored to be the carrier of your fiery bolt message.
A question needs to be asked...
Inquiring minds want to know...
Can you say unequivocally you have no hand in the Pottawatomie Massacre?

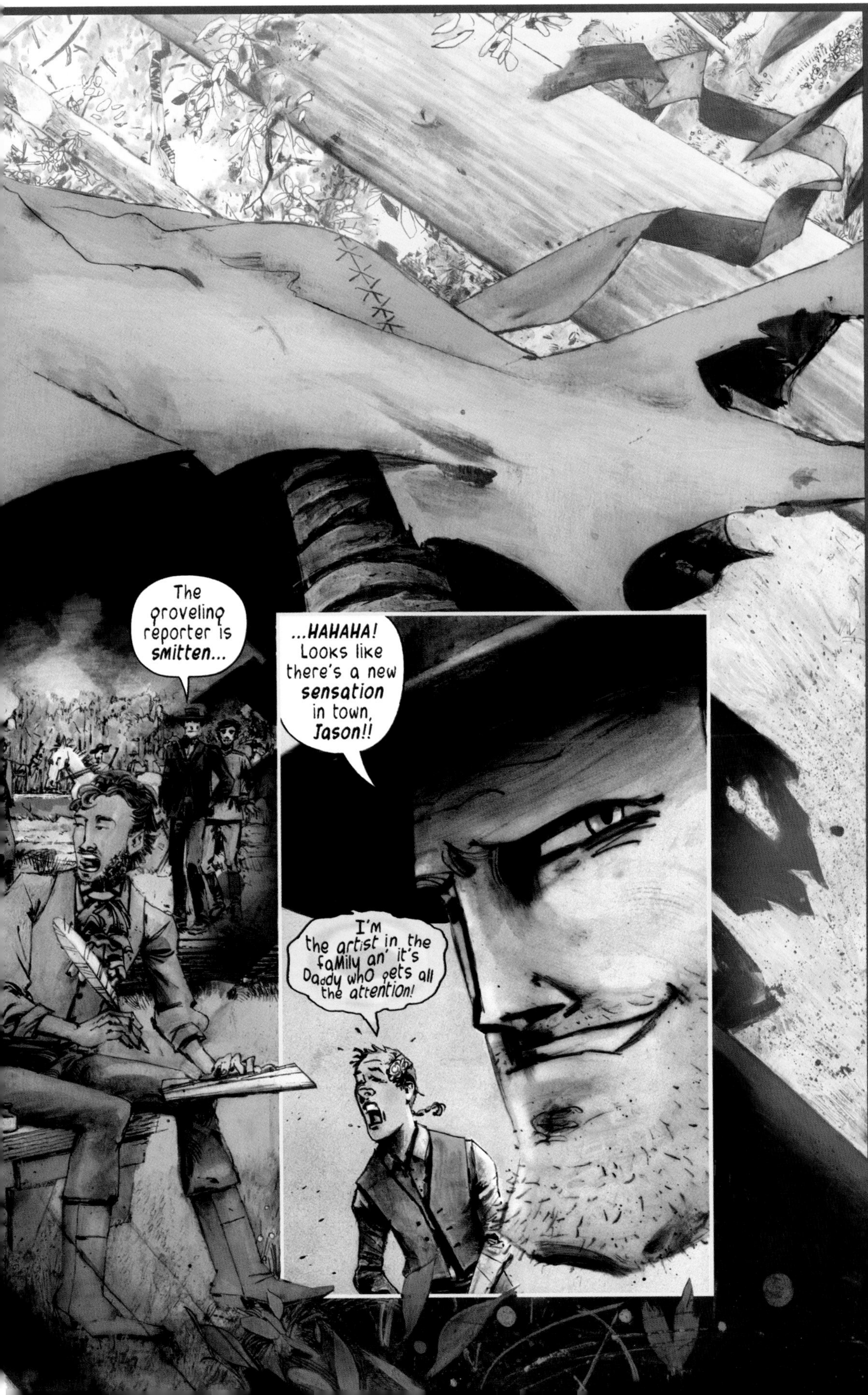
The groveling reporter is smitten...
...HAHAHA! Looks like there's a new sensation in town, Jason!!
I'm the artist in the family an' it's Daddy who gets all the attention!

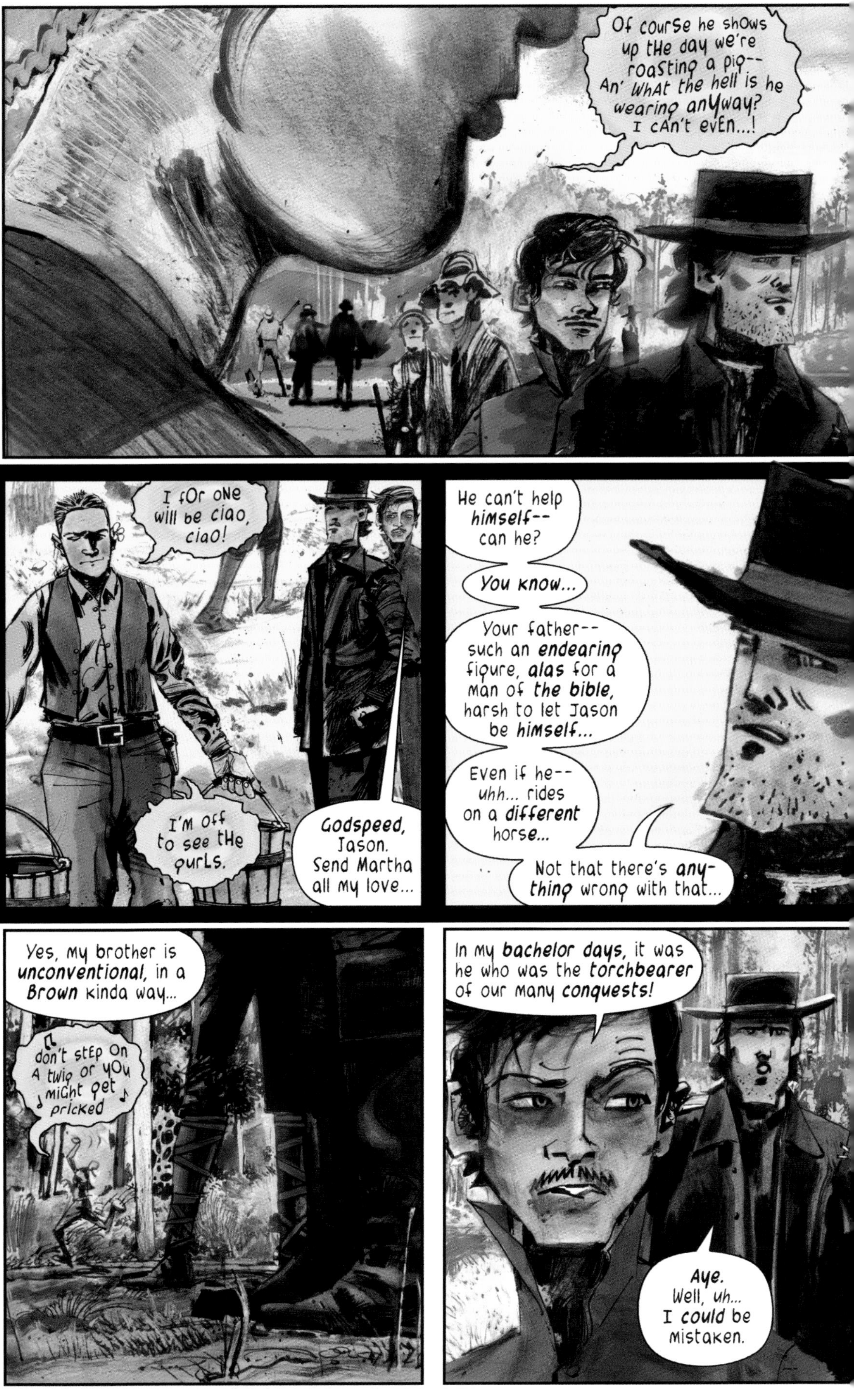
Of course he shows up the day we're roasting a pig-- An' what the hell is he wearing anyway? I can't even...!
I for one will be ciao, ciao!
I'm off to see the gurls.
Godspeed, Jason. Send Martha all my love...
He can't help himself-- can he?
You know...
Your father-- such an endearing figure, alas for a man of the bible, harsh to let Jason be himself...
Even if he-- uhh... rides on a different horse...
Not that there's anything wrong with that...
Yes, my brother is unconventional, in a Brown kinda way...
don't step on a twig or you might get pricked
In my bachelor days, it was he who was the torchbearer of our many conquests!
Aye. Well, uh... I could be mistaken.

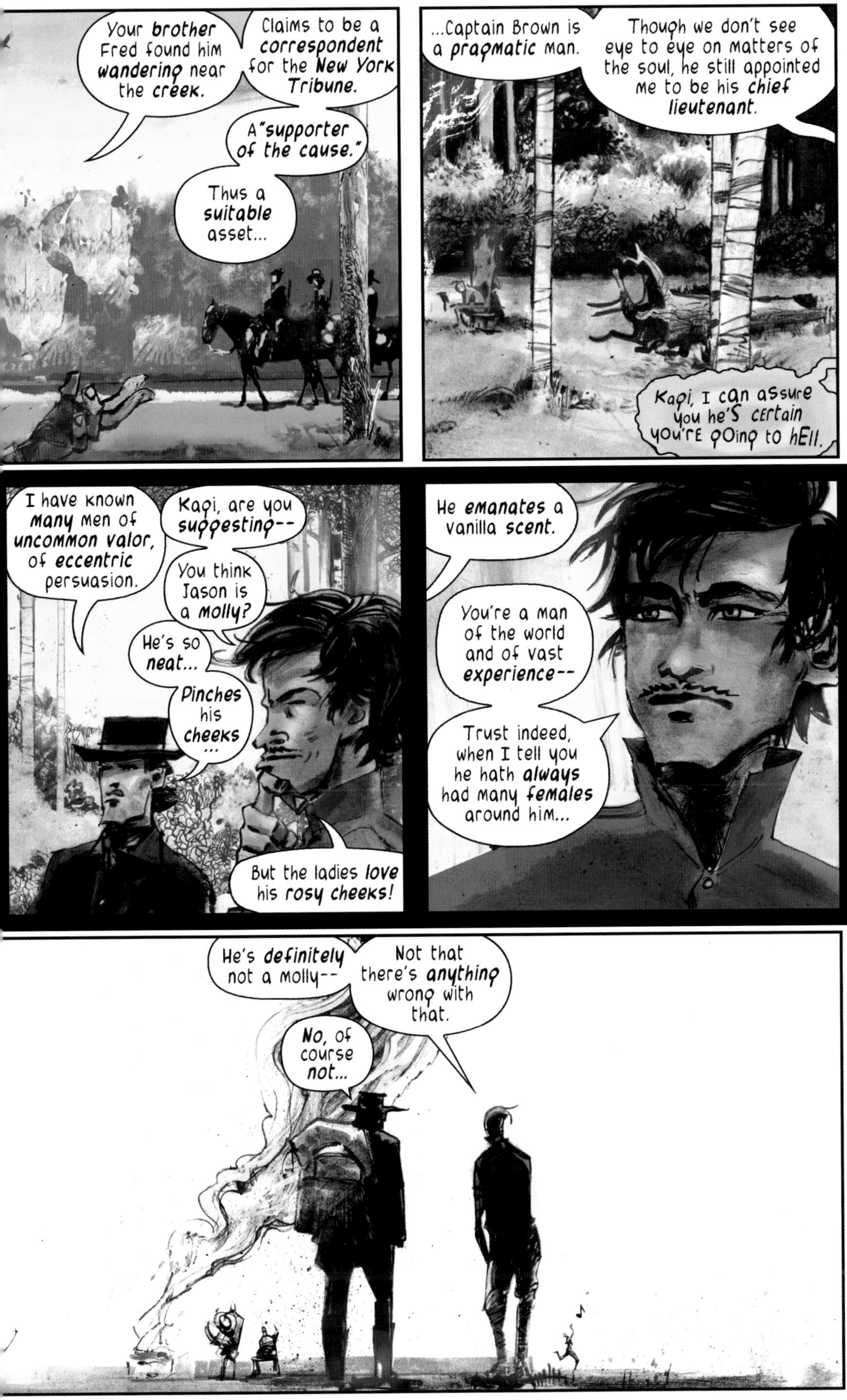

Your brother Fred found him wandering near the creek.
Claims to be a correspondent for the New York Tribune.
A "supporter of the cause."
Thus a suitable asset...
...Captain Brown is a pragmatic man.
Though we don't see eye to eye on matters of the soul, he still appointed me to be his chief lieutenant.
Kagi, I can assure you he's certain you're going to hell.
I have known many men of uncommon valor, of eccentric persuasion.
Kagi, are you suggesting--
You think Jason is a molly?
He's so neat...
Pinches his cheeks...
But the ladies love his rosy cheeks!
He emanates a vanilla scent.
You're a man of the world and of vast experience--
Trust indeed, when I tell you he hath always had many females around him...
He's definitely not a molly--
Not that there's anything wrong with that.
No, of course not...

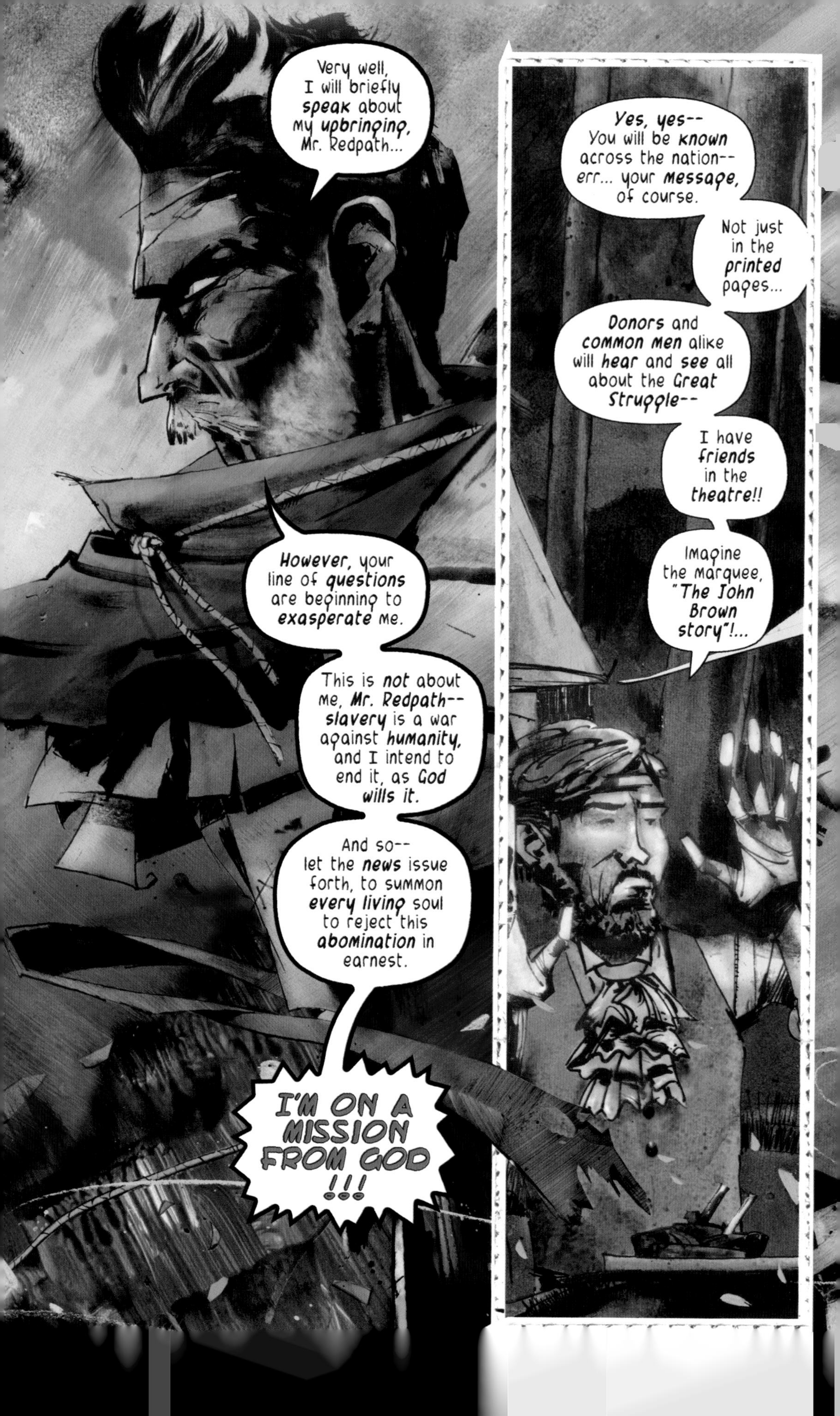
Very well, I will briefly speak about my upbringing, Mr. Redpath...
However, your line of questions are beginning to exasperate me.
This is not about me, Mr. Redpath-- slavery is a war against humanity, and I intend to end it, as God wills it.
And so-- let the news issue forth, to summon every living soul to reject this abomination in earnest.
I'M ON A MISSION FROM GOD !!!
Yes, yes-- You will be known across the nation-- err... your message, of course.
Not just in the printed pages...
Donors and common men alike will hear and see all about the Great Struggle--
I have friends in the theatre!!
Imagine the marquee, "The John Brown story"!...

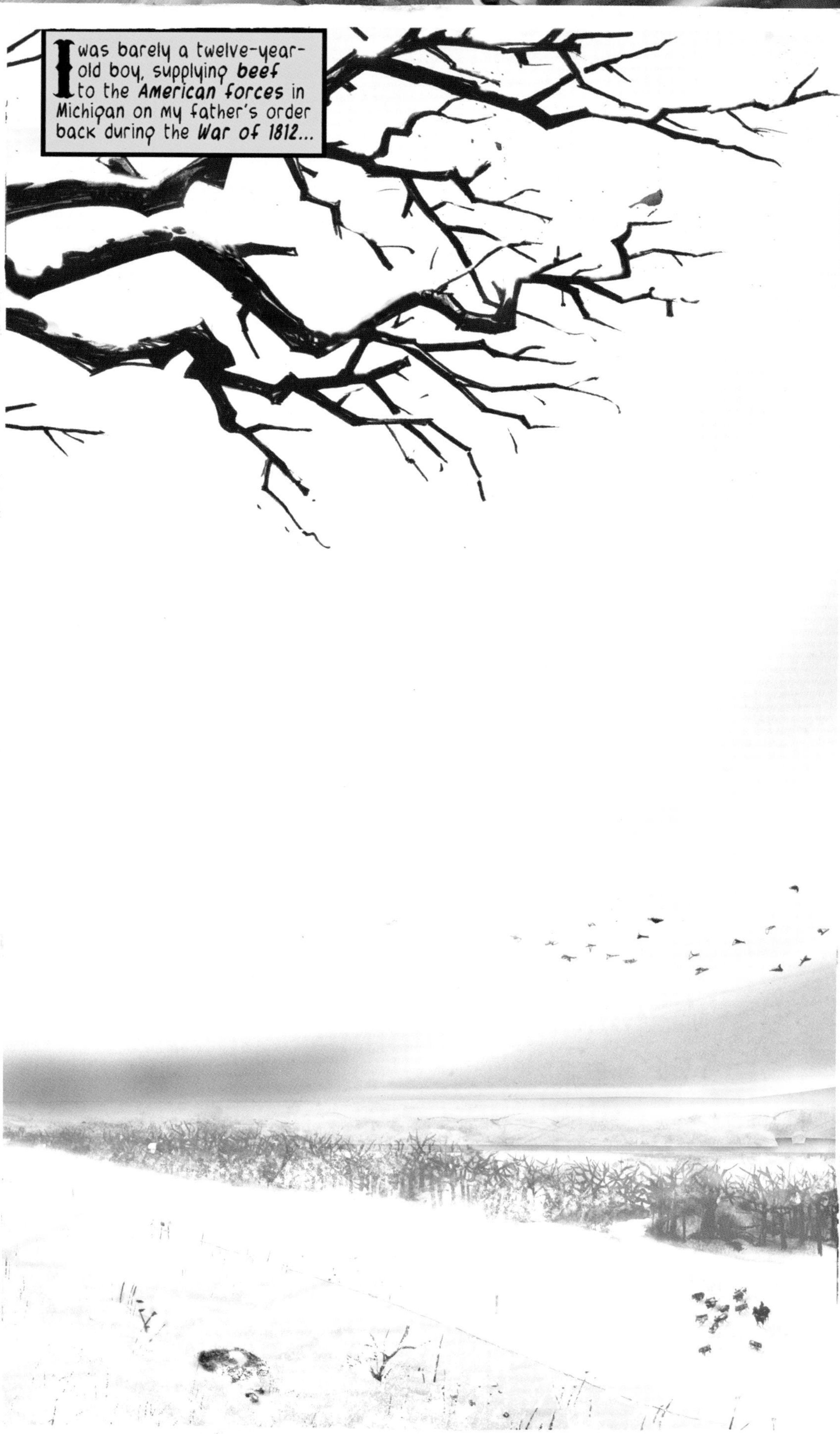
I was barely a twelve-year-old boy, supplying beef to the American forces in Michigan on my father's order back during the War of 1812...

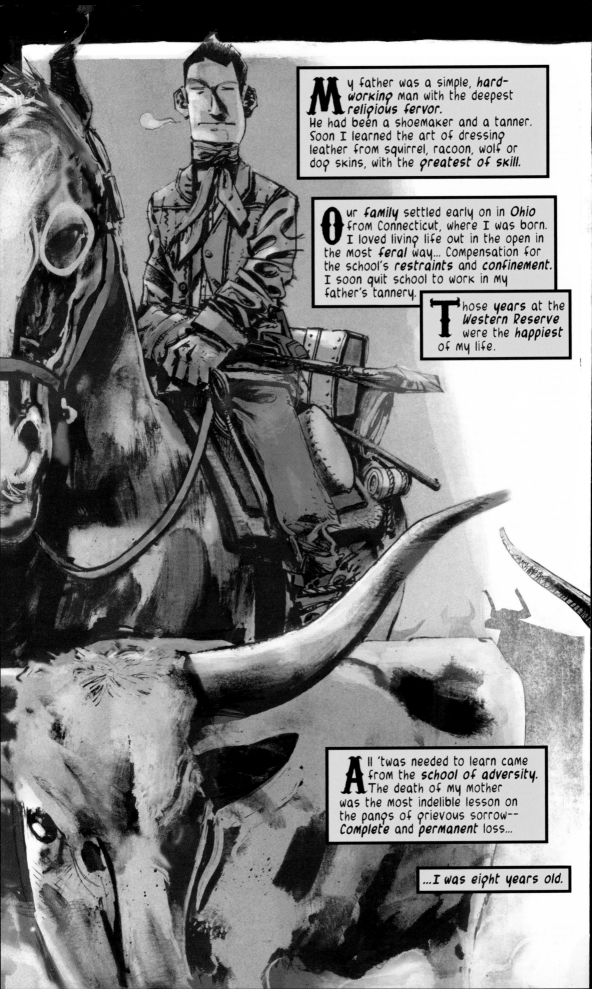

My father was a simple, *hard-working* man with the deepest *religious fervor.*
He had been a shoemaker and a tanner. Soon I learned the art of dressing leather from squirrel, racoon, wolf or dog skins, with the *greatest of skill.*

Our *family* settled early on in *Ohio* from Connecticut, where I was born. I loved living life out in the open in the most *feral way...* Compensation for the school's *restraints* and *confinement.* I soon quit school to work in my father's tannery.

Those *years* at the *Western Reserve* were the *happiest* of my life.

All 'twas needed to learn came from the *school of adversity.* The death of my mother was the most indelible lesson on the pangs of grievous sorrow-- *Complete* and *permanent* loss...

...I was *eight years old.*

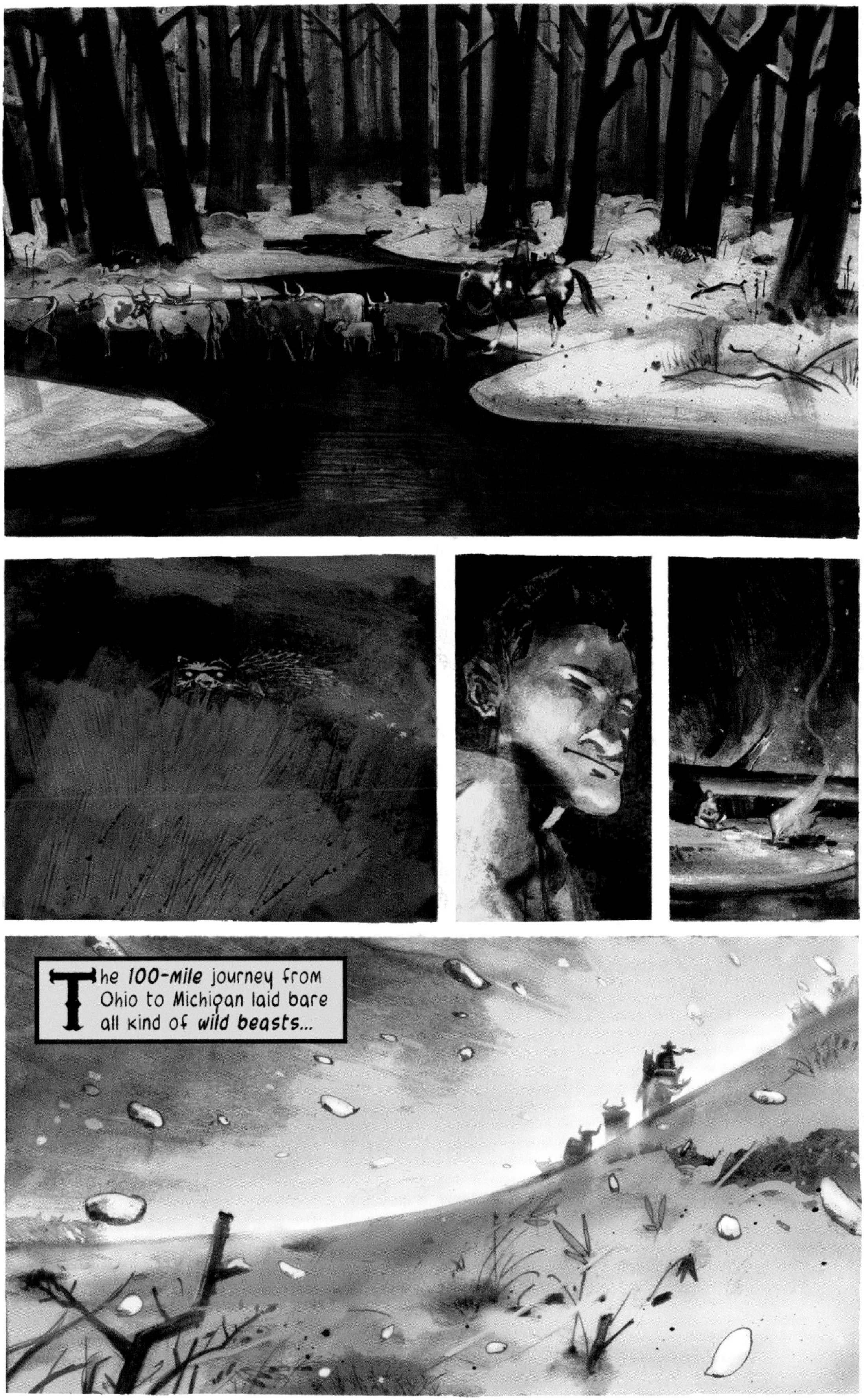
The 100-mile journey from Ohio to Michigan laid bare all kind of wild beasts...

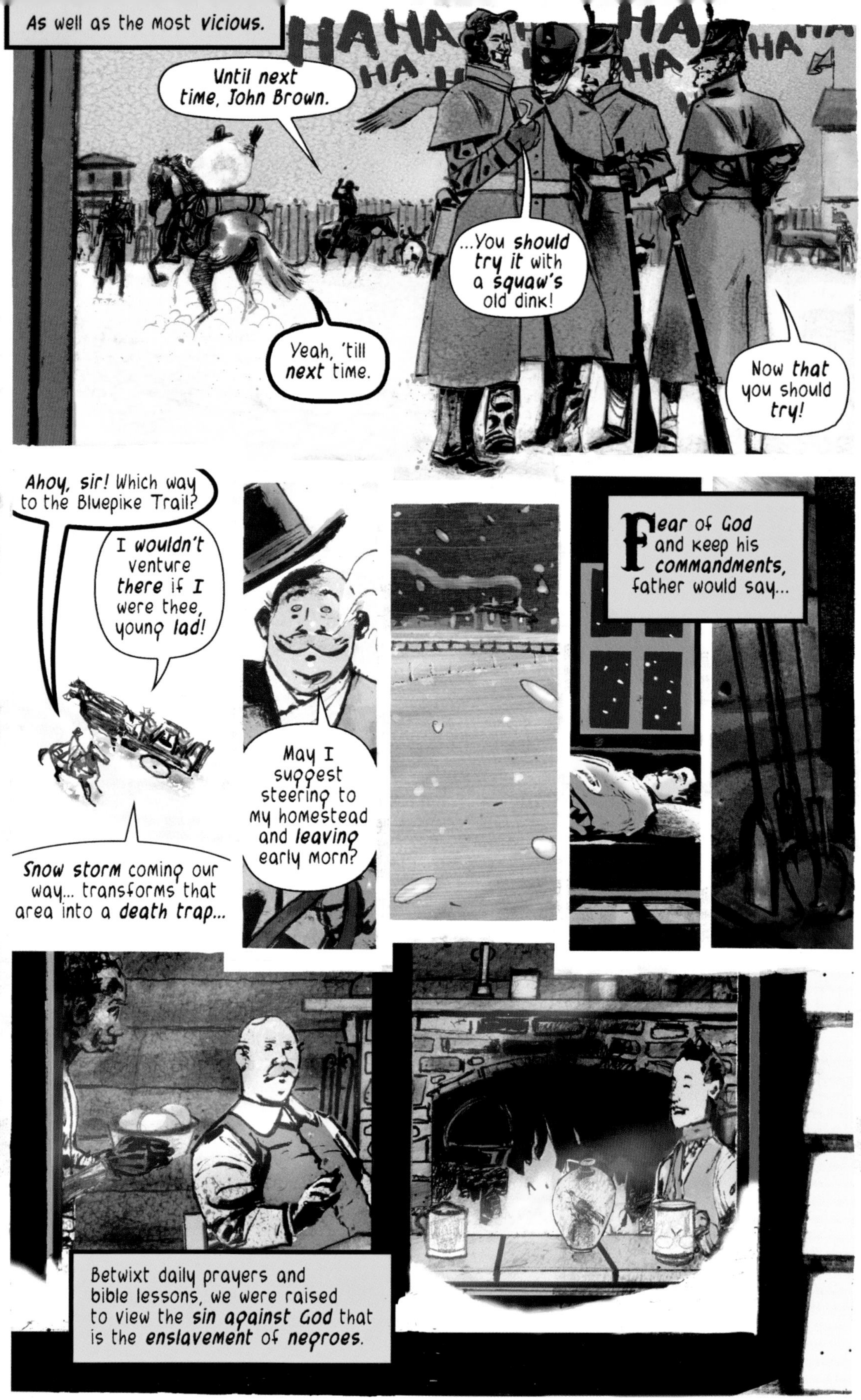
As well as the most vicious.
HAHAHAHA HA HA HA HA
Until next time, John Brown.
...You should try it with a squaw's old dink!
Yeah, 'till next time.
Now that you should try!
Ahoy, sir! Which way to the Bluepike Trail?
I wouldn't venture there if I were thee, young lad!
Snow storm coming our way... transforms that area into a death trap...
May I suggest steering to my homestead and leaving early morn?
Fear of God and keep his commandments, father would say...
Betwixt daily prayers and bible lessons, we were raised to view the sin against God that is the enslavement of negroes.

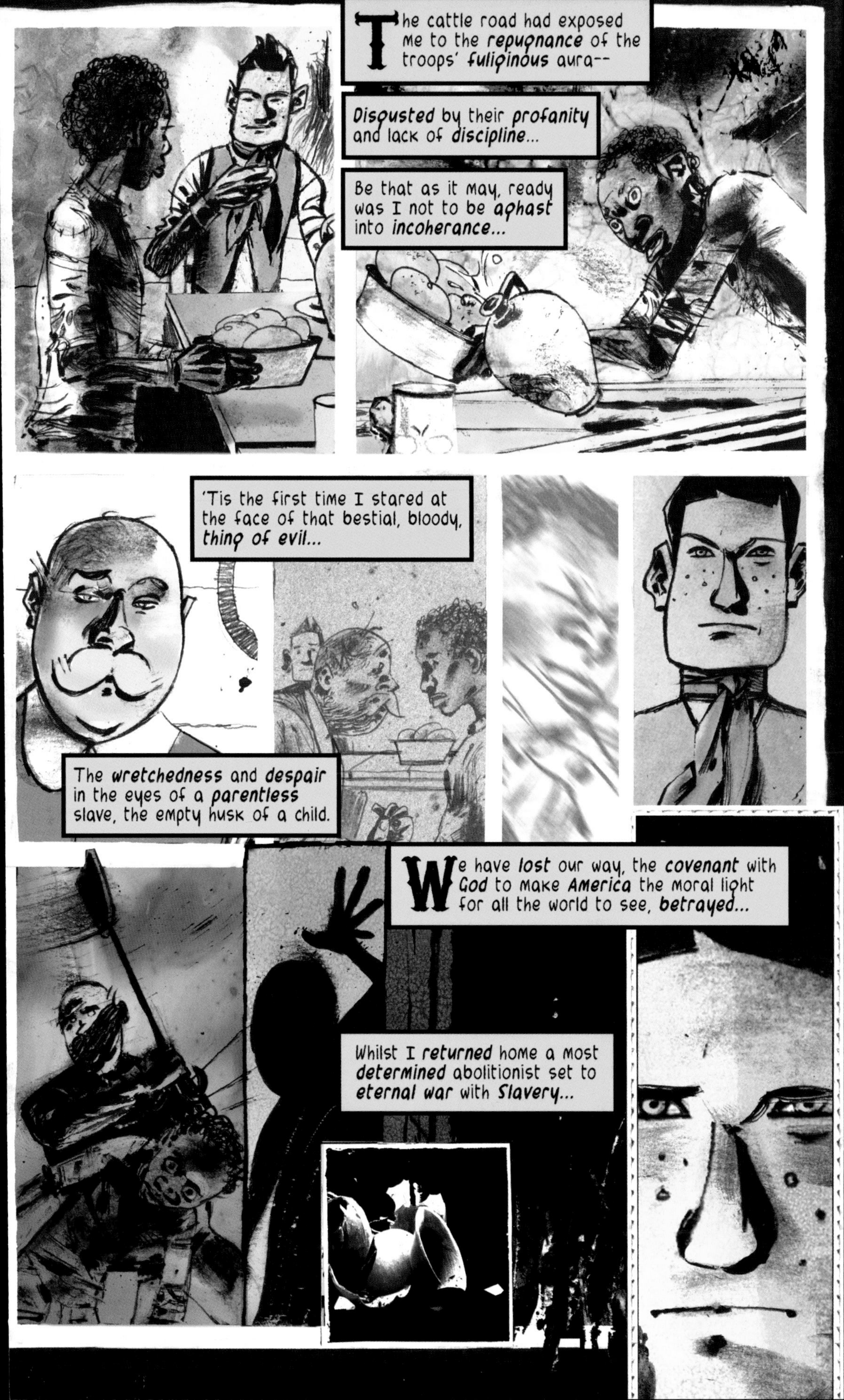
The cattle road had exposed me to the repugnance of the troops' fuliginous aura--
Disgusted by their profanity and lack of discipline...
Be that as it may, ready was I not to be aghast into incoherance...
'Tis the first time I stared at the face of that bestial, bloody, thing of evil...
The wretchedness and despair in the eyes of a parentless slave, the empty husk of a child.
We have lost our way, the covenant with God to make America the moral light for all the world to see, betrayed...
Whilst I returned home a most determined abolitionist set to eternal war with Slavery...

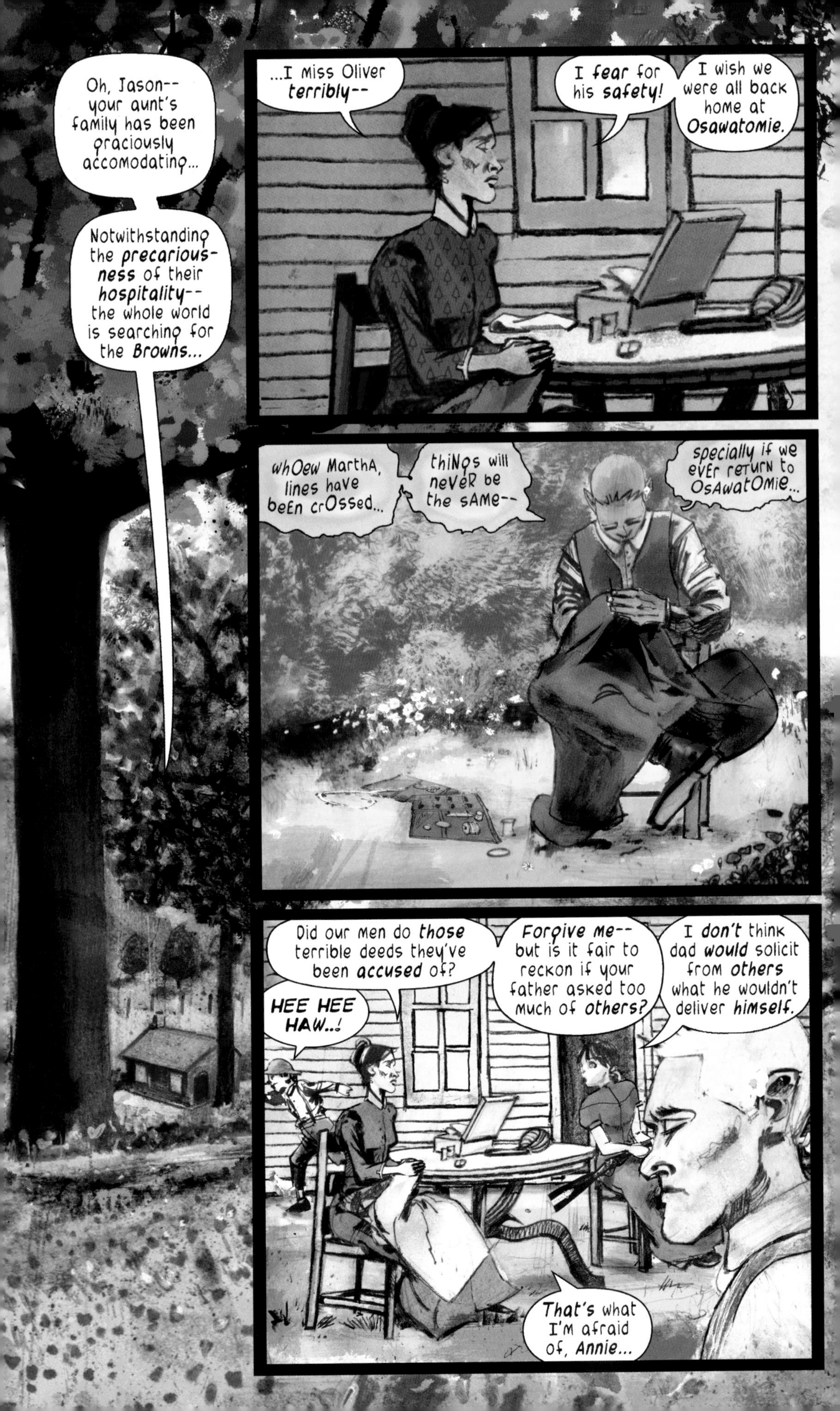
Oh, Jason-- your aunt's family has been graciously accomodating...
Notwithstanding the *precariousness* of their *hospitality*-- the whole world is searching for the *Browns*...
...I miss Oliver *terribly*--
I *fear* for his *safety*!
I wish we were all back home at *Osawatomie.*
whOew MarthA, lines have beEn crOssed...
thiNgs will neveR be the sAME--
specially if we evEr return to OsAwatOmie...
Did our men do *those* terrible deeds they've been *accused* of?
HEE HEE HAW..!
Forgive me-- but is it fair to reckon if your father asked too much of *others*?
I *don't* think dad *would* solicit from *others* what he wouldn't deliver *himself*.
That's what I'm afraid of, *Annie*...

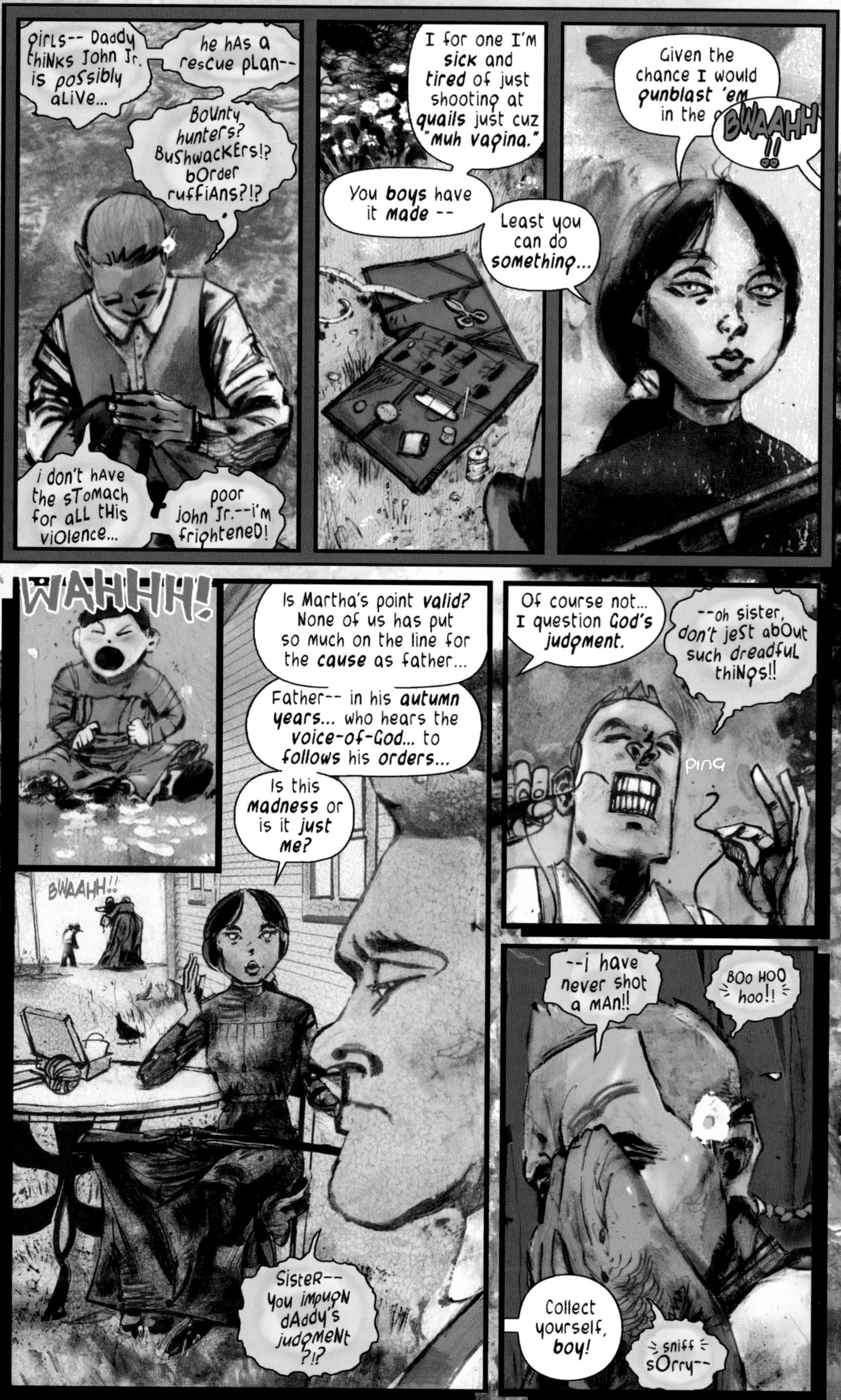
girls-- Daddy thinks John Jr. is possibly alive...
he has a rescue plan--
Bounty hunters? Bushwackers!? border ruffians?!?
i don't have the stomach for all this violence...
poor john Jr.--i'm frightened!
I for one I'm sick and tired of just shooting at quails just cuz "muh vagina."
You boys have it made --
Least you can do something...
Given the chance I would gunblast 'em in the
BWAAHH!!
WAHHH!
Is Martha's point valid? None of us has put so much on the line for the cause as father...
Father-- in his autumn years... who hears the voice-of-God... to follows his orders...
Is this madness or is it just me?
BWAAHH!!
Sister-- You impugn daddy's judgment ?!?
Of course not... I question God's judgment.
--oh sister, don't jest about such dreadful things!!
ping
--i have never shot a man!!
Boo hoo hoo!!
Collect yourself, boy!
sniff sorry--

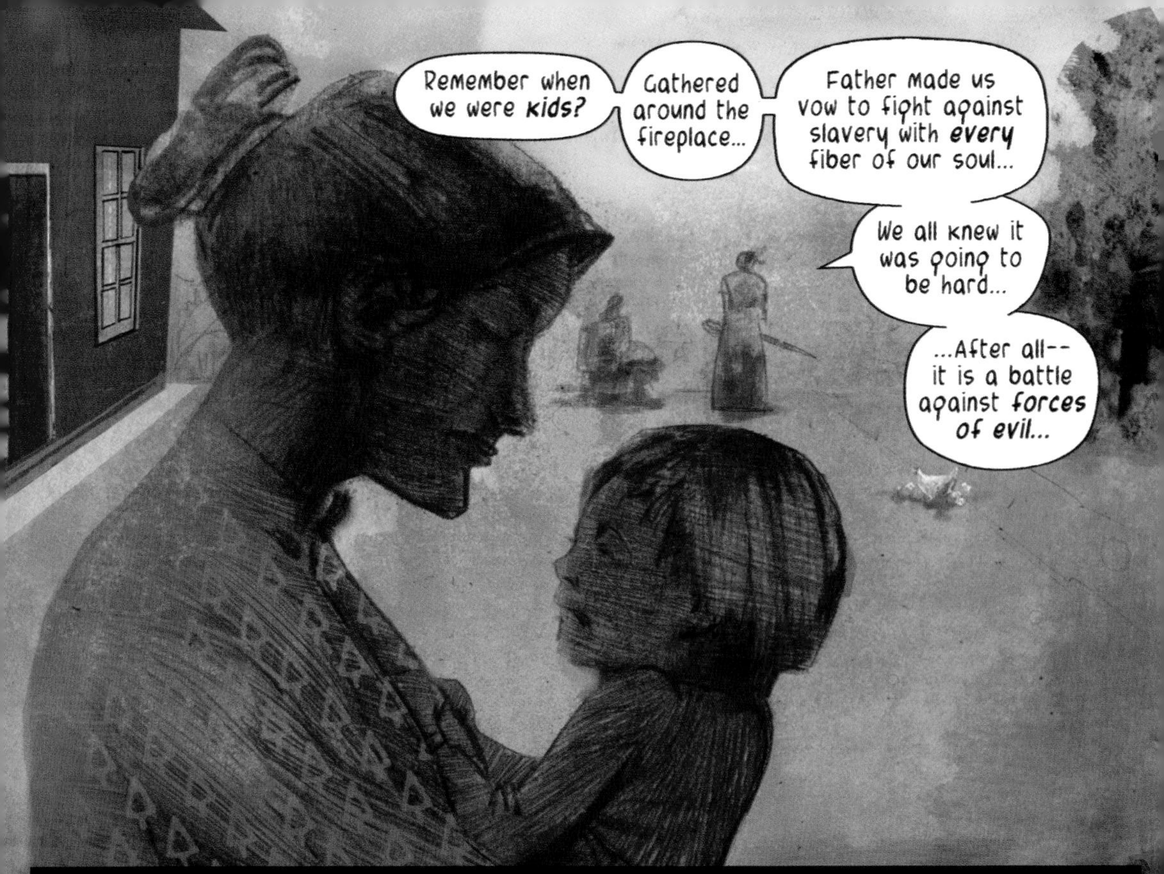

Remember when we were kids?
Gathered around the fireplace...
Father made us vow to fight against slavery with every fiber of our soul...
We all knew it was going to be hard...
...After all-- it is a battle against forces of evil...

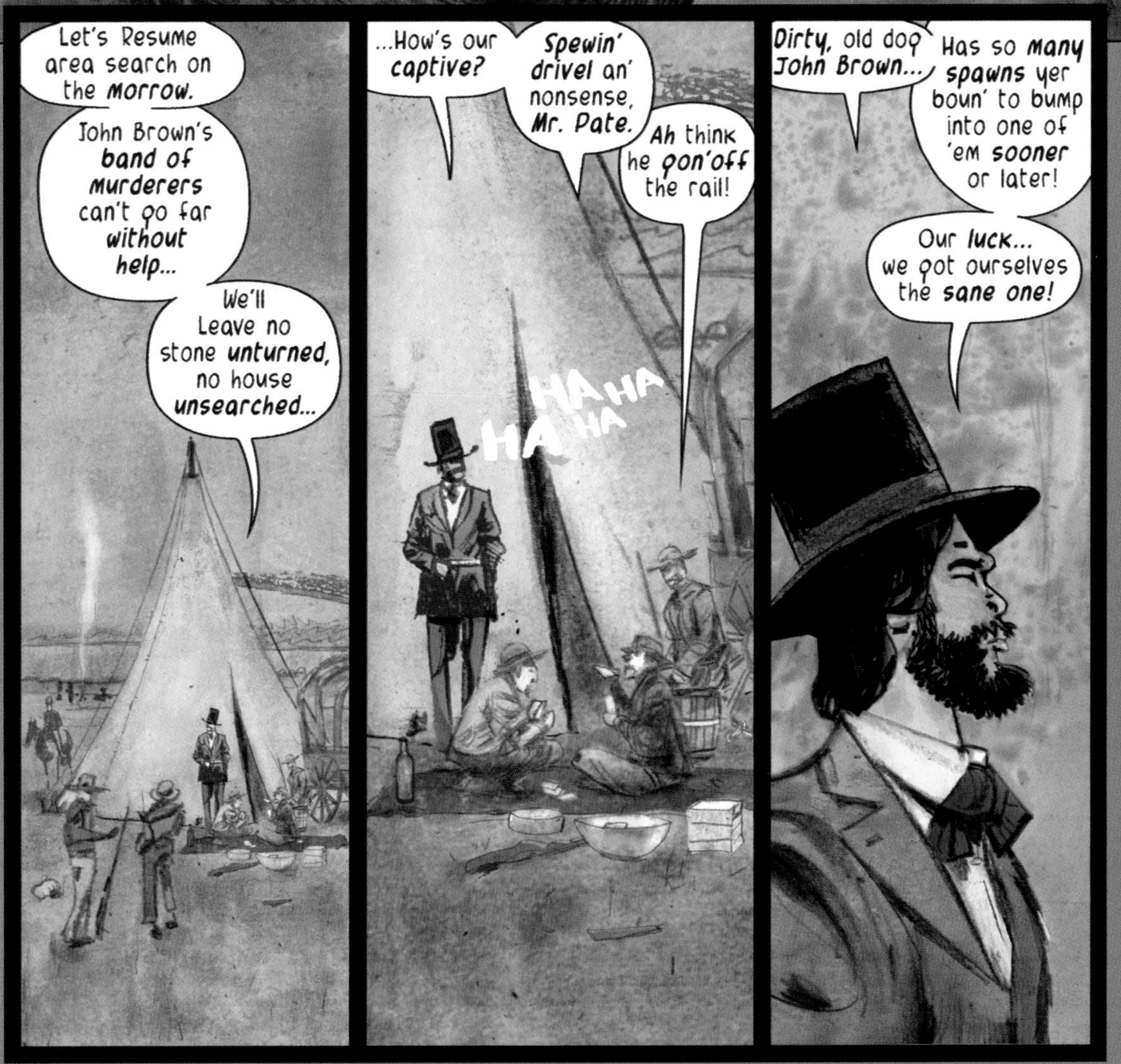

Let's Resume area search on the morrow.
John Brown's band of murderers can't go far without help...
We'll Leave no stone unturned, no house unsearched...
...How's our captive?
Spewin' drivel an' nonsense, Mr. Pate.
Ah think he gon'off the rail!
HA HA HA HA
Dirty, old dog John Brown...
Has so many spawns yer boun' to bump into one of 'em sooner or later!
Our luck... we got ourselves the sane one!

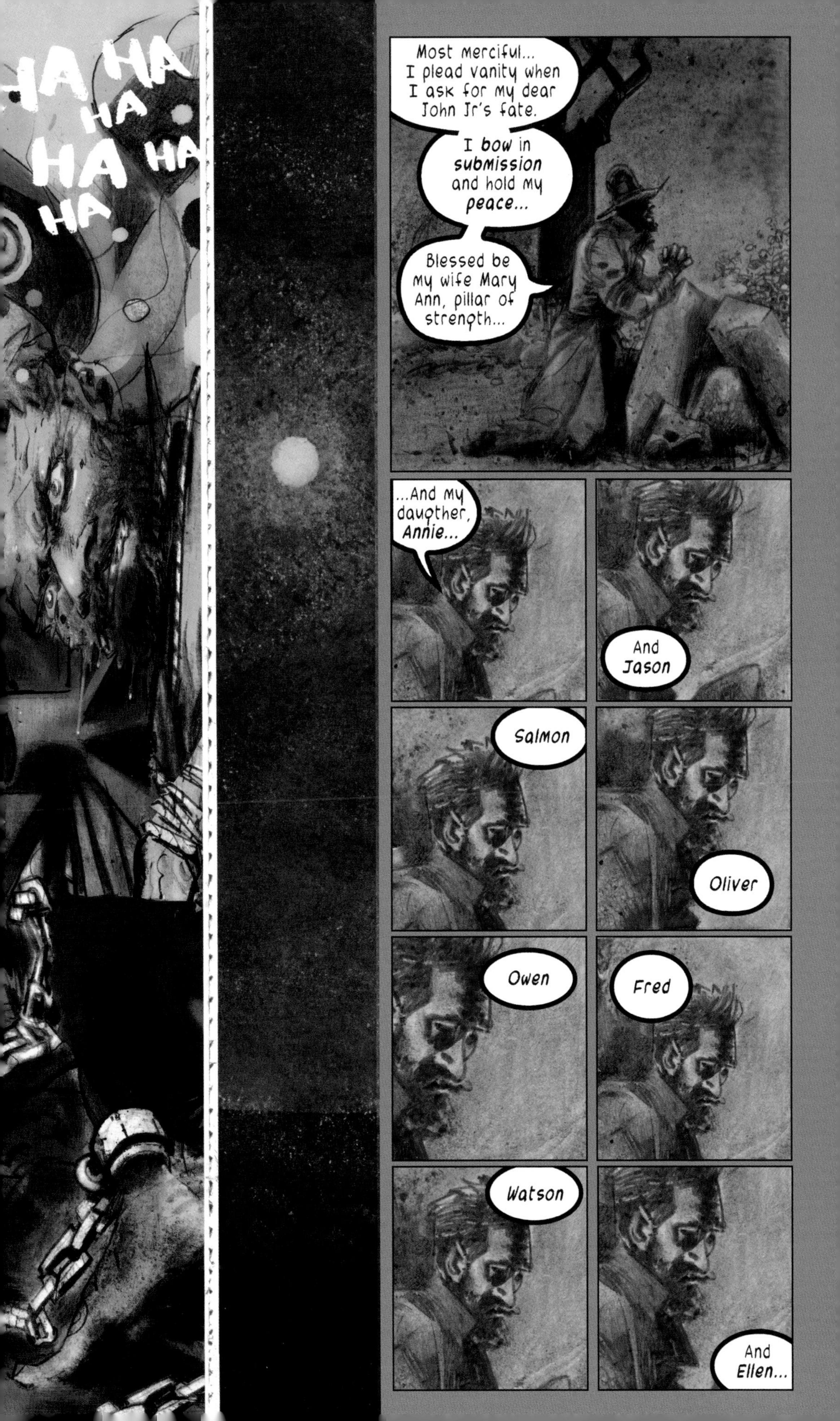
HA HA HA HA HA HA
Most merciful... I plead vanity when I ask for my dear John Jr's fate.
I bow in submission and hold my peace...
Blessed be my wife Mary Ann, pillar of strength...
...And my daughter, Annie...
And Jason
Salmon
Oliver
Owen
Fred
Watson
And Ellen...

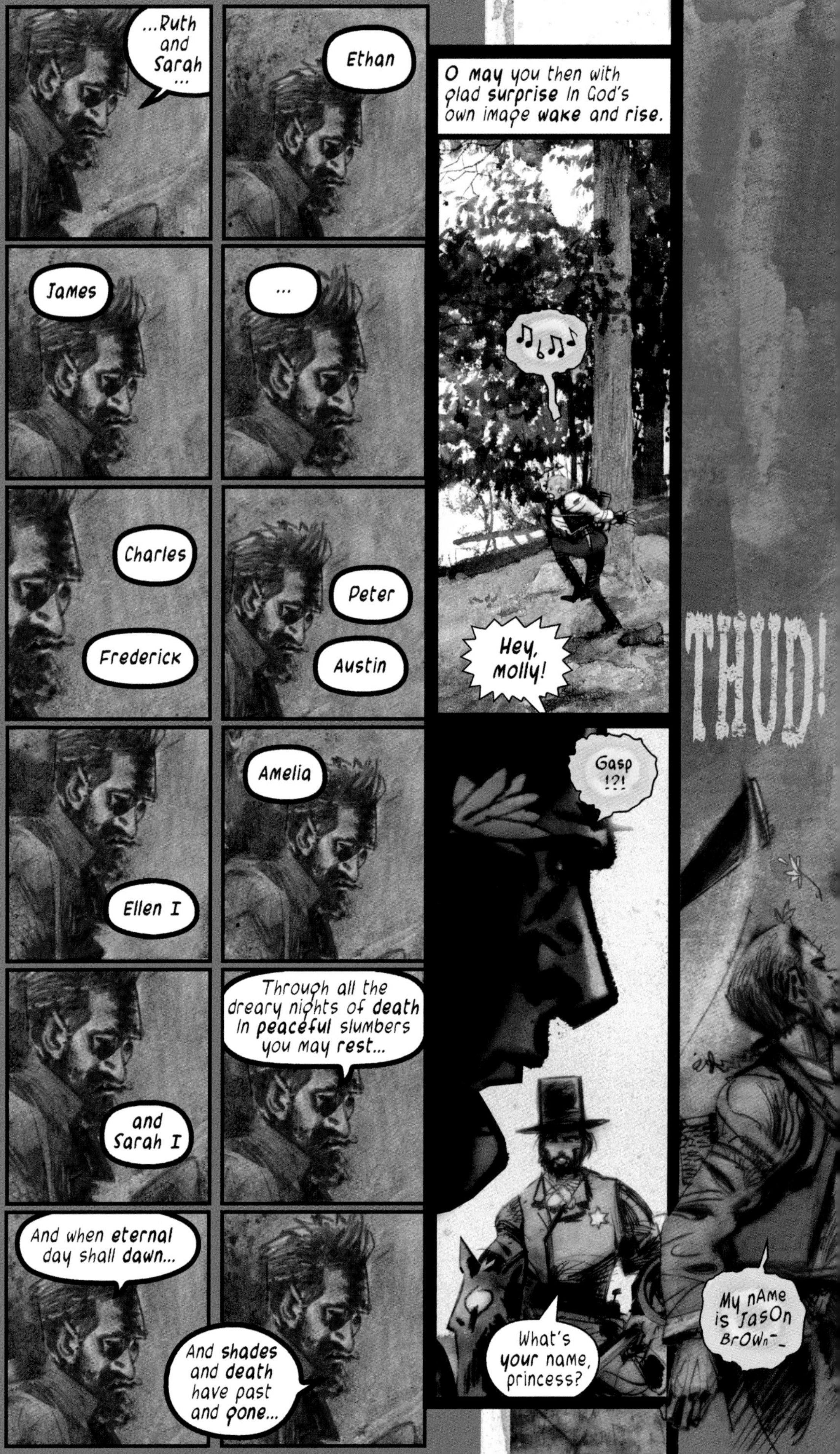

...Ruth and Sarah ...
Ethan
James
...
Charles
Frederick
Peter
Austin
Ellen I
Amelia
and Sarah I
Through all the dreary nights of death In peaceful slumbers you may rest...
And when eternal day shall dawn...
And shades and death have past and gone...
O may you then with glad surprise In God's own image wake and rise.
Hey, molly!
Gasp !?!
What's your name, princess?
THUD!
My nAme is JasOn BrOwn-_

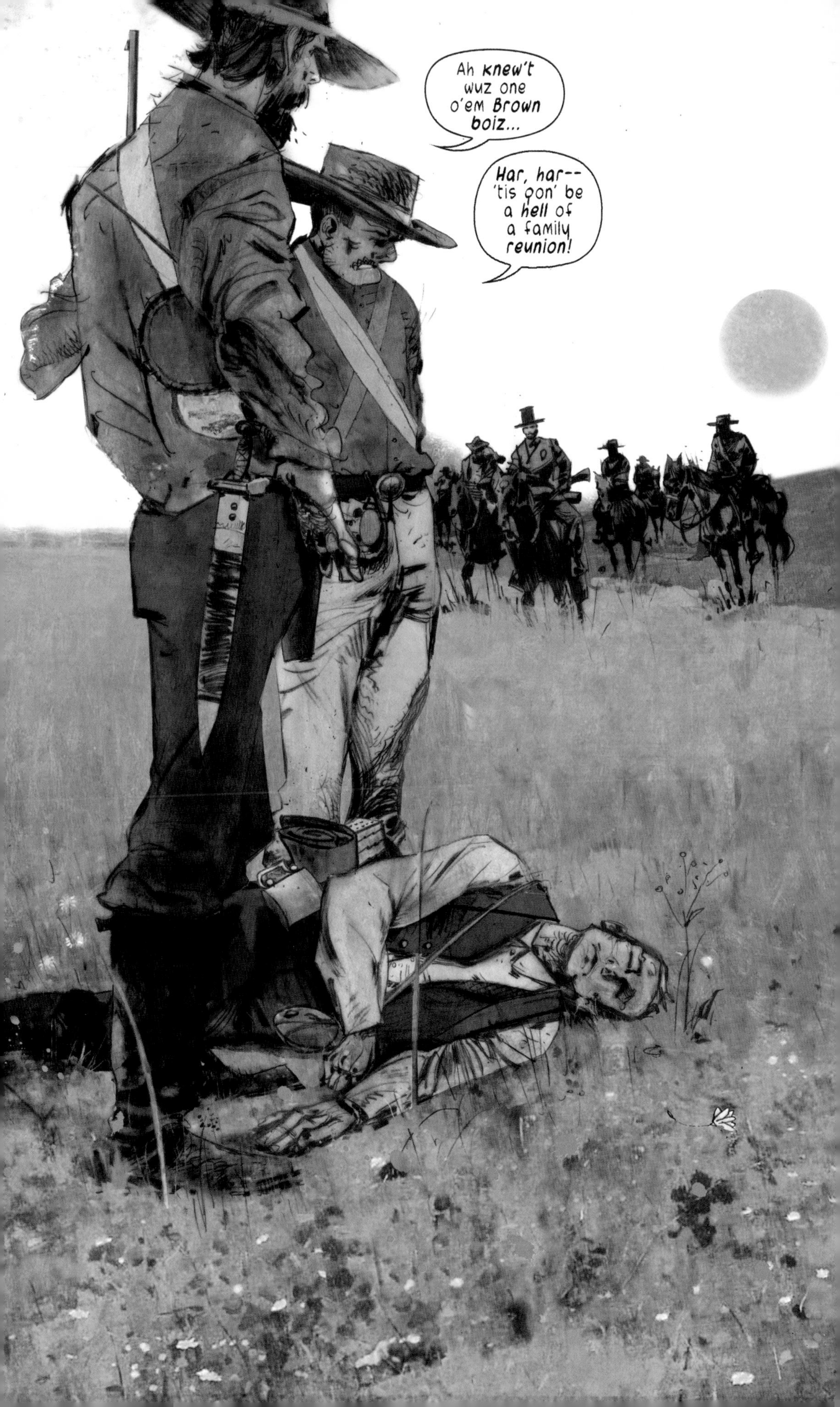
Ah knew't wuz one o'em Brown boiz...
Har, har-- 'tis gon' be a hell of a family reunion!

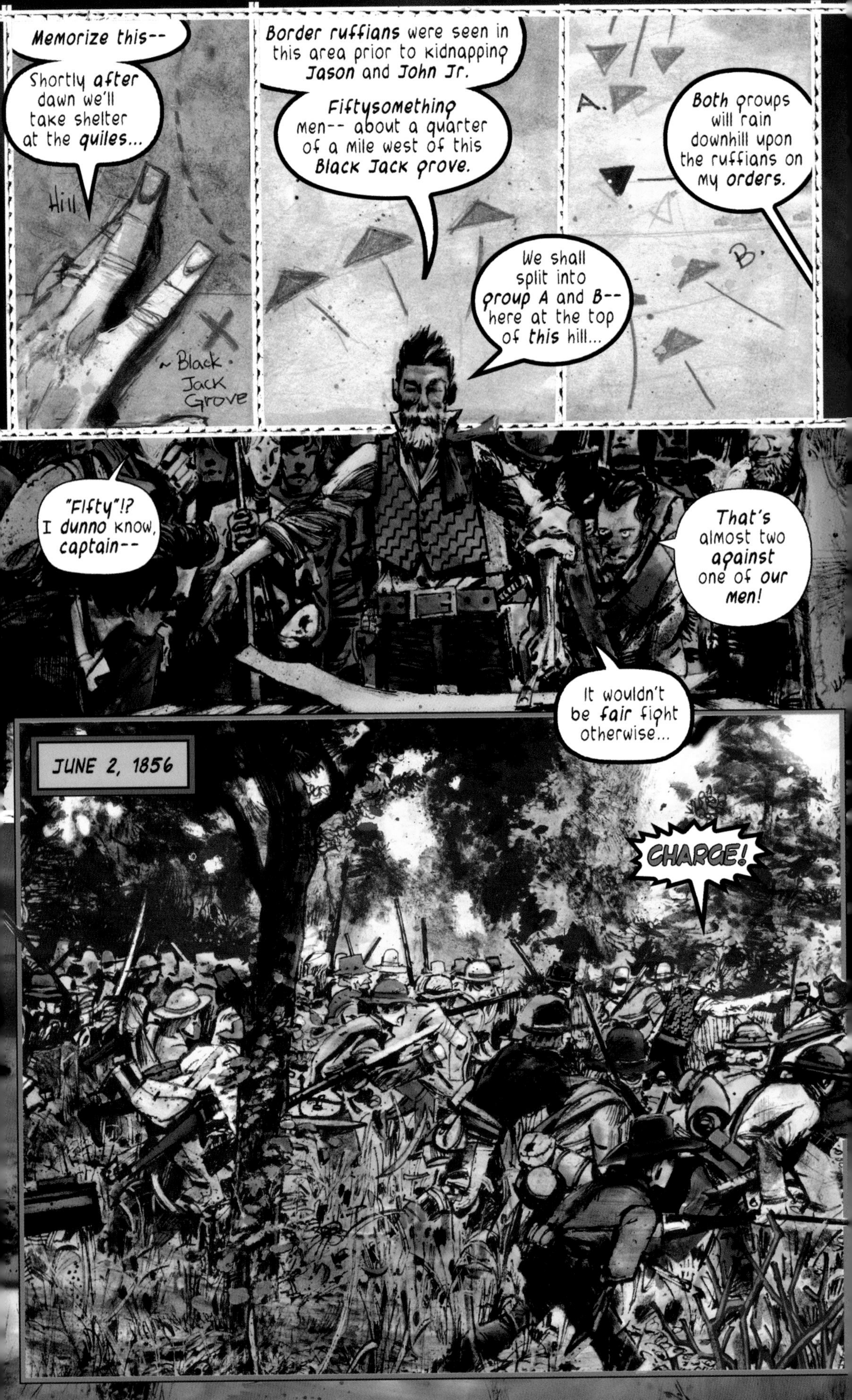
Memorize this--
Shortly after dawn we'll take shelter at the quiles...
Hill
Black Jack Grove
Border ruffians were seen in this area prior to kidnapping Jason and John Jr.
Fiftysomething men-- about a quarter of a mile west of this Black Jack grove.
We shall split into group A and B-- here at the top of this hill...
A.
B.
Both groups will rain downhill upon the ruffians on my orders.
"Fifty"!? I dunno know, captain--
That's almost two against one of our men!
It wouldn't be fair fight otherwise...
JUNE 2, 1856
CHARGE!

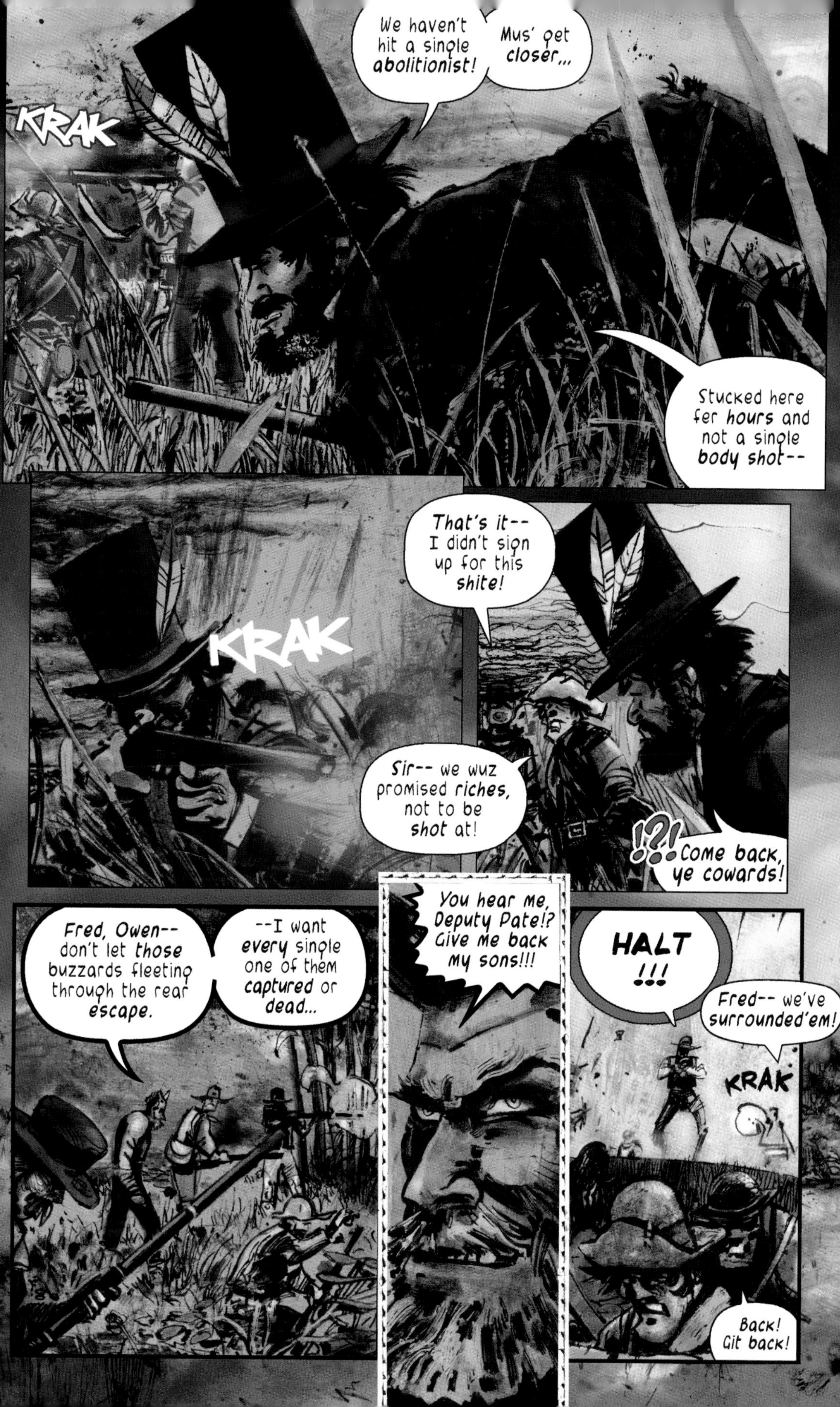
KRAK
We haven't hit a single abolitionist!
Mus' get closer...
Stucked here fer hours and not a single body shot--
KRAK
That's it-- I didn't sign up for this shite!
Sir-- we wuz promised riches, not to be shot at!
!?!
Come back, ye cowards!
Fred, Owen-- don't let those buzzards fleeting through the rear escape.
--I want every single one of them captured or dead...
You hear me, Deputy Pate!? Give me back my sons!!!
HALT !!!
Fred-- we've surrounded'em!
KRAK
Back! Git back!

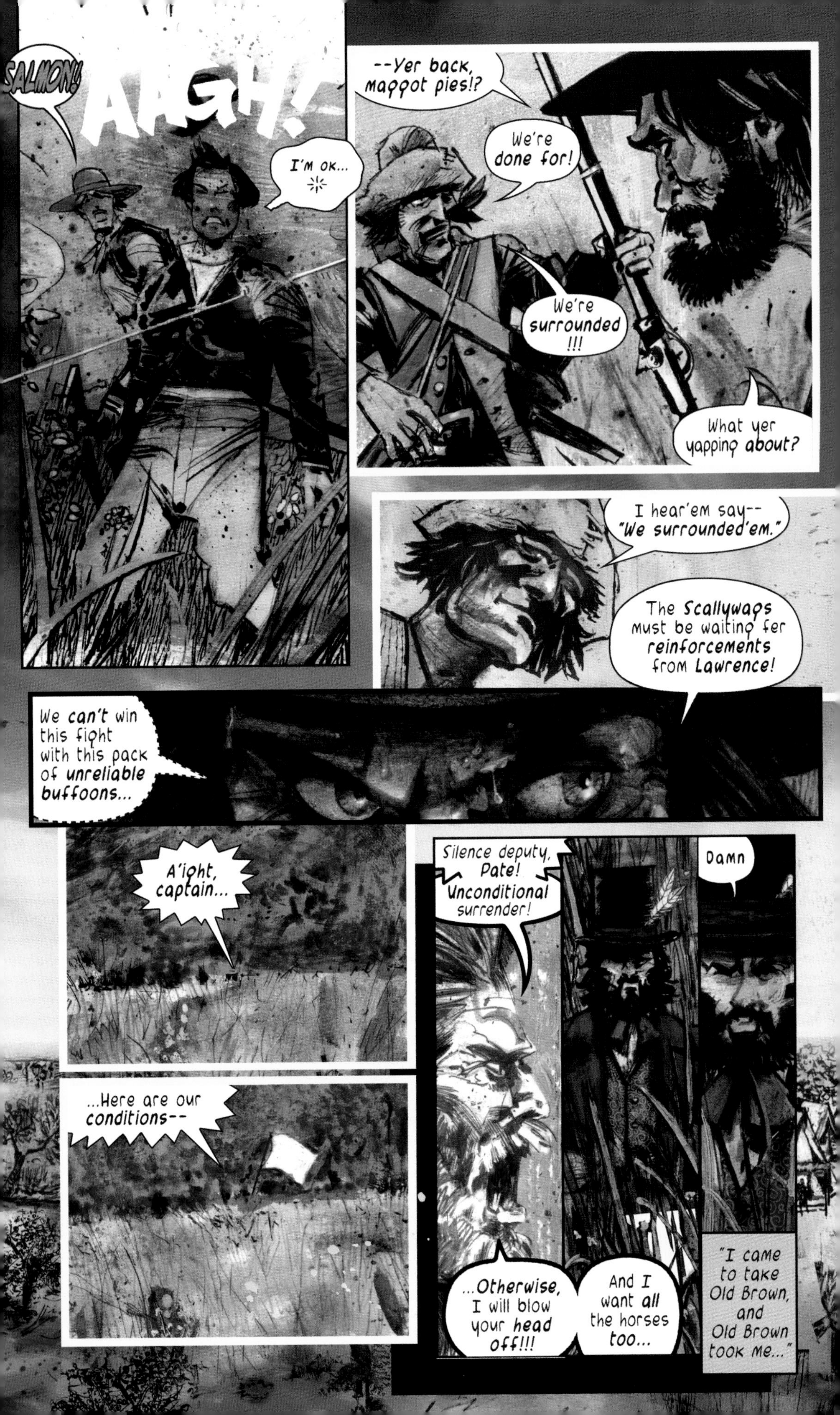
SALMON!
AAGH!
I'M OK...
--Yer back, maggot pies!?
We're done for!
We're surrounded !!!
What yer yapping about?
I hear'em say-- "We surrounded'em."
The Scallywags must be waiting fer reinforcements from Lawrence!
We can't win this fight with this pack of unreliable buffoons...
A'ight, captain...
...Here are our conditions--
Silence deputy, Pate! Unconditional surrender!
Damn
...Otherwise, I will blow your head off!!!
And I want all the horses too...
"I came to take Old Brown, and Old Brown took me..."

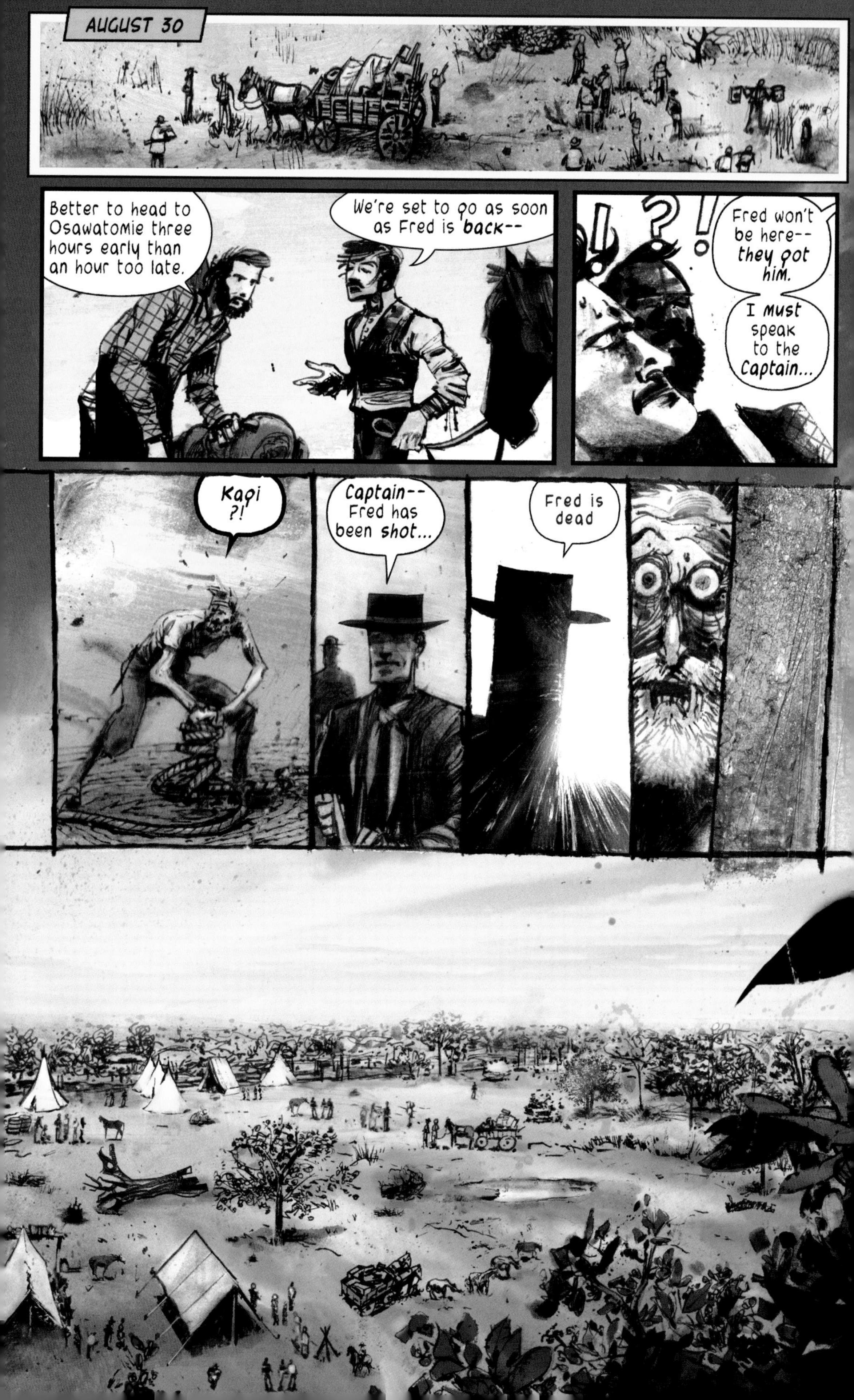
AUGUST 30
Better to head to Osawatomie three hours early than an hour too late.
We're set to go as soon as Fred is back--
!?!
Fred won't be here-- they got him.
I must speak to the Captain...
Kagi ?!
Captain-- Fred has been shot...
Fred is dead

3

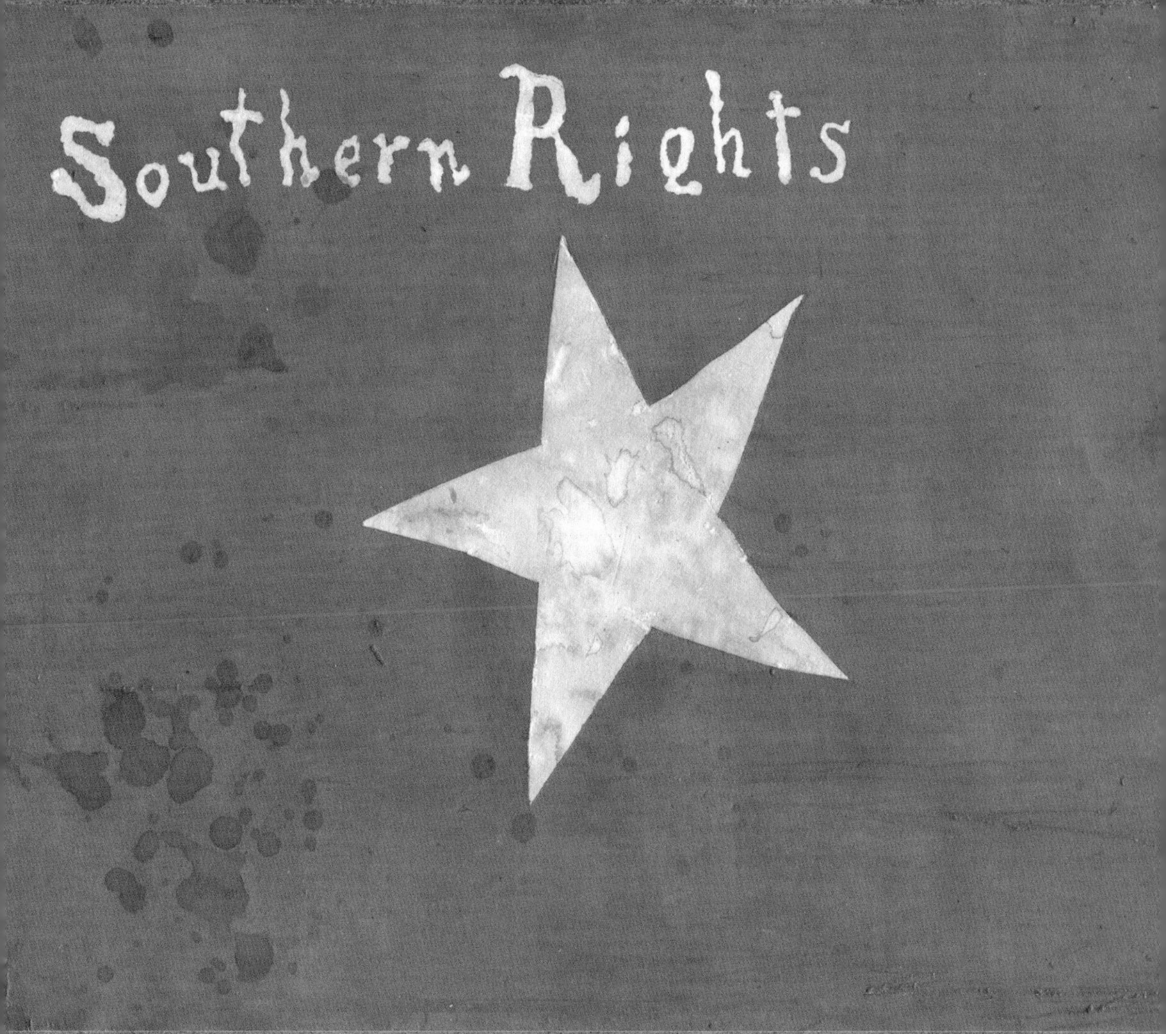
Southern Rights

ON TREACHEROUS GROUND

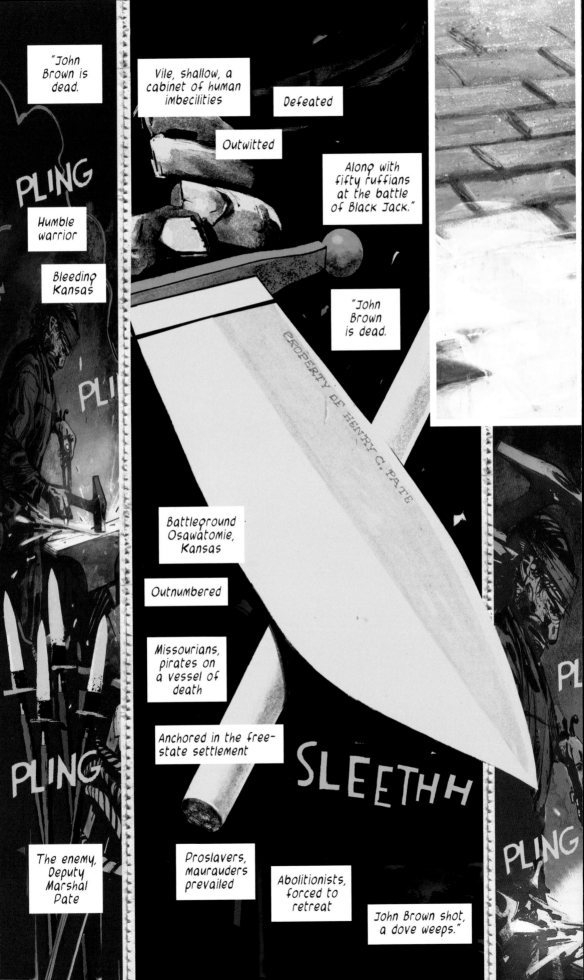

"John Brown is dead.

PLING

Humble warrior

Bleeding Kansas

PLI

PLING

Vile, shallow, a cabinet of human imbecilities

Defeated

Outwitted

Along with fifty ruffians at the battle of Black Jack."

"John Brown is dead.

Battleground Osawatomie, Kansas

Outnumbered

Missourians, pirates on a vessel of death

Anchored in the free-state settlement

SLEETHH

PROPERTY OF HENRY C. PATE

PL

PLING

The enemy, Deputy Marshal Pate

Proslavers, maurauders prevailed

Abolitionists, forced to retreat

John Brown shot, a dove weeps."

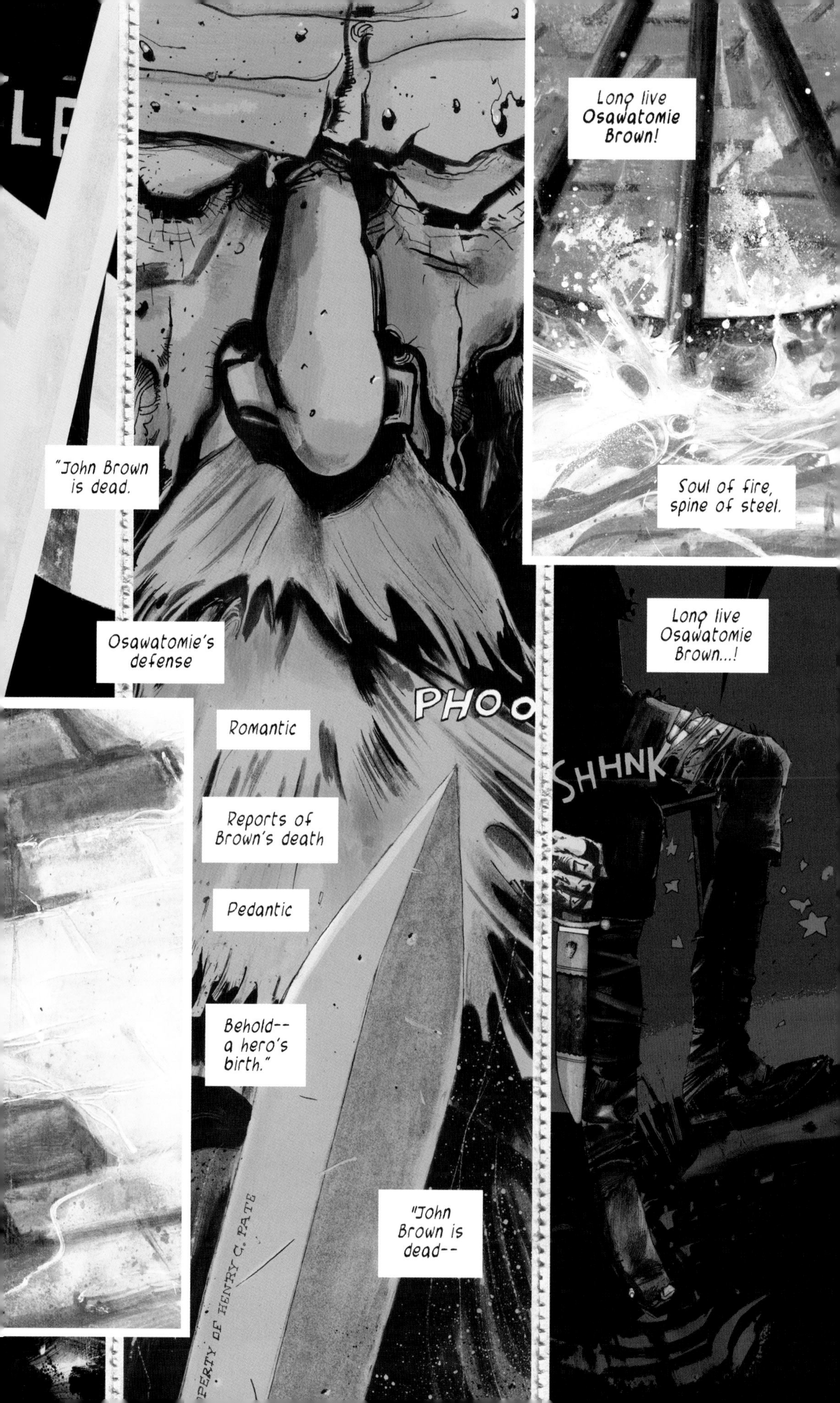
"John Brown is dead.
Osawatomie's defense
Romantic
Reports of Brown's death
Pedantic
Behold-- a hero's birth."
PHOO
PERTY OF HENRY C. PATE
"John Brown is dead--
Long live Osawatomie Brown!
Soul of fire, spine of steel.
Long live Osawatomie Brown...!
SHHNK

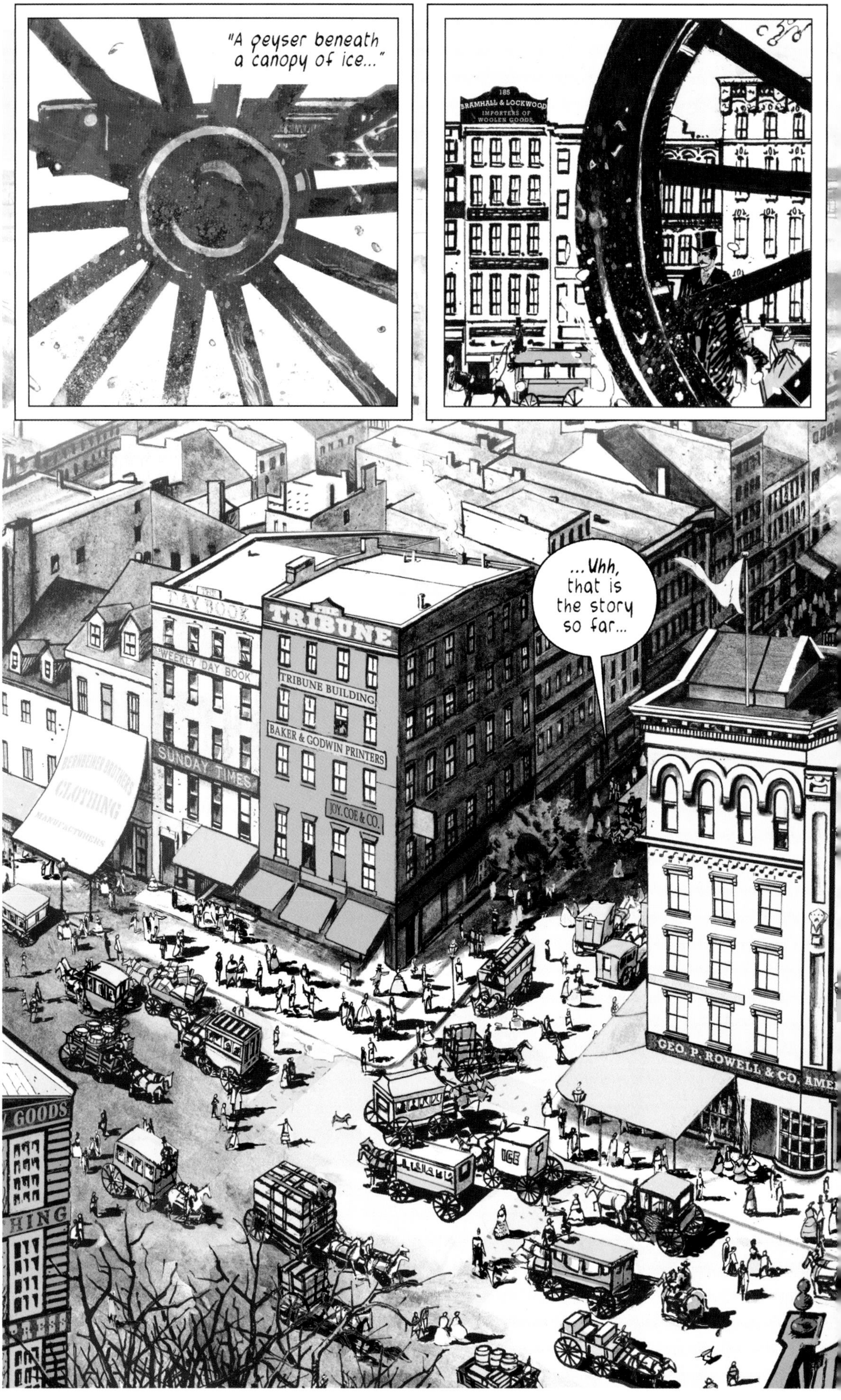
"A geyser beneath a canopy of ice..."
185
BRAMHALL & LOCKWOOD
IMPORTERS OF WOOLEN GOODS
THE DAY BOOK
WEEKLY DAY BOOK
SUNDAY TIMES
THE TRIBUNE
TRIBUNE BUILDING
BAKER & GODWIN PRINTERS
JOY, COE & CO.
BERNHEIMER BROTHERS
CLOTHING
MANUFACTURERS
...Uhh, that is the story so far...
ICE
GEO. P. ROWELL & CO.

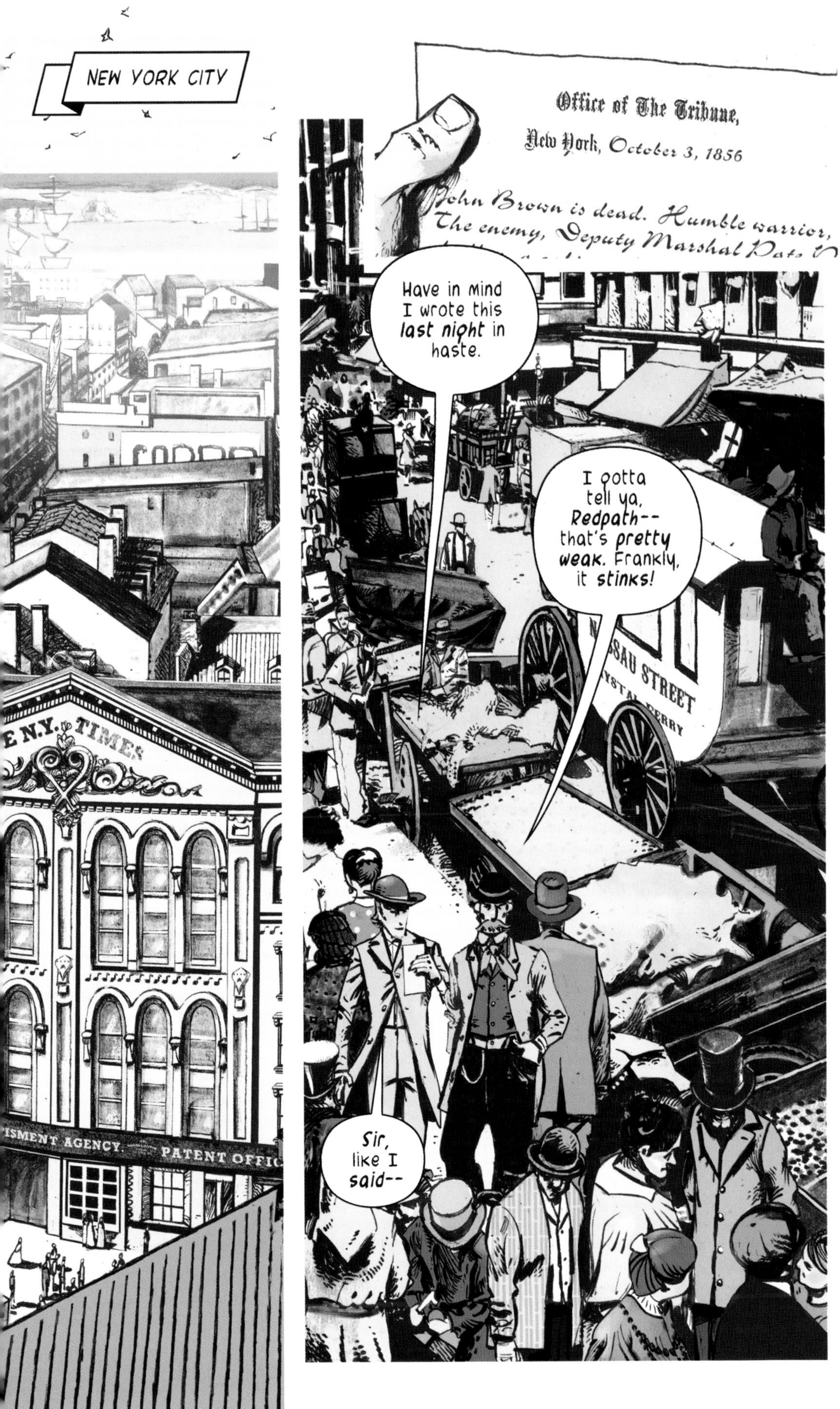
NEW YORK CITY
N.Y. TIMES
PATENT
Office of The Tribune,
New York, October 3, 1856
John Brown is dead. Humble warrior,
The enemy, Deputy Marshal
Have in mind I wrote this *last night* in haste.
I gotta tell ya, *Redpath*-- that's *pretty weak*. Frankly, it *stinks!*
Sir, like I *said*--

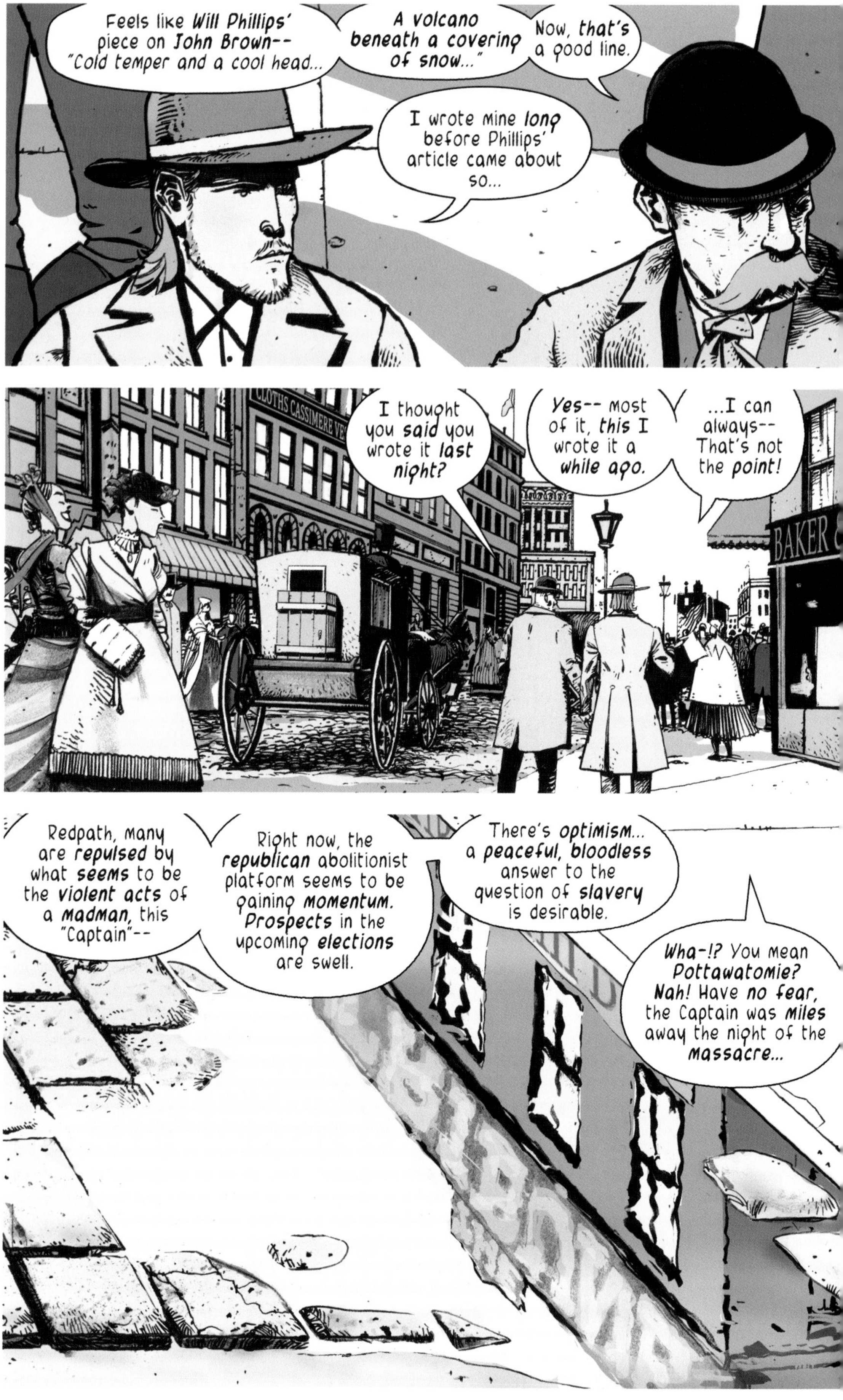

Feels like Will Phillips' piece on John Brown-- "Cold temper and a cool head...
A volcano beneath a covering of snow..."
Now, that's a good line.
I wrote mine long before Phillips' article came about so...
CLOTHS CASSIMERE VE
I thought you said you wrote it last night?
Yes-- most of it, this I wrote it a while ago.
...I can always-- That's not the point!
BAKER
Redpath, many are repulsed by what seems to be the violent acts of a madman, this "Captain"--
Right now, the republican abolitionist platform seems to be gaining momentum. Prospects in the upcoming elections are swell.
There's optimism... a peaceful, bloodless answer to the question of slavery is desirable.
Wha-!? You mean Pottawatomie? Nah! Have no fear, the Captain was miles away the night of the massacre...

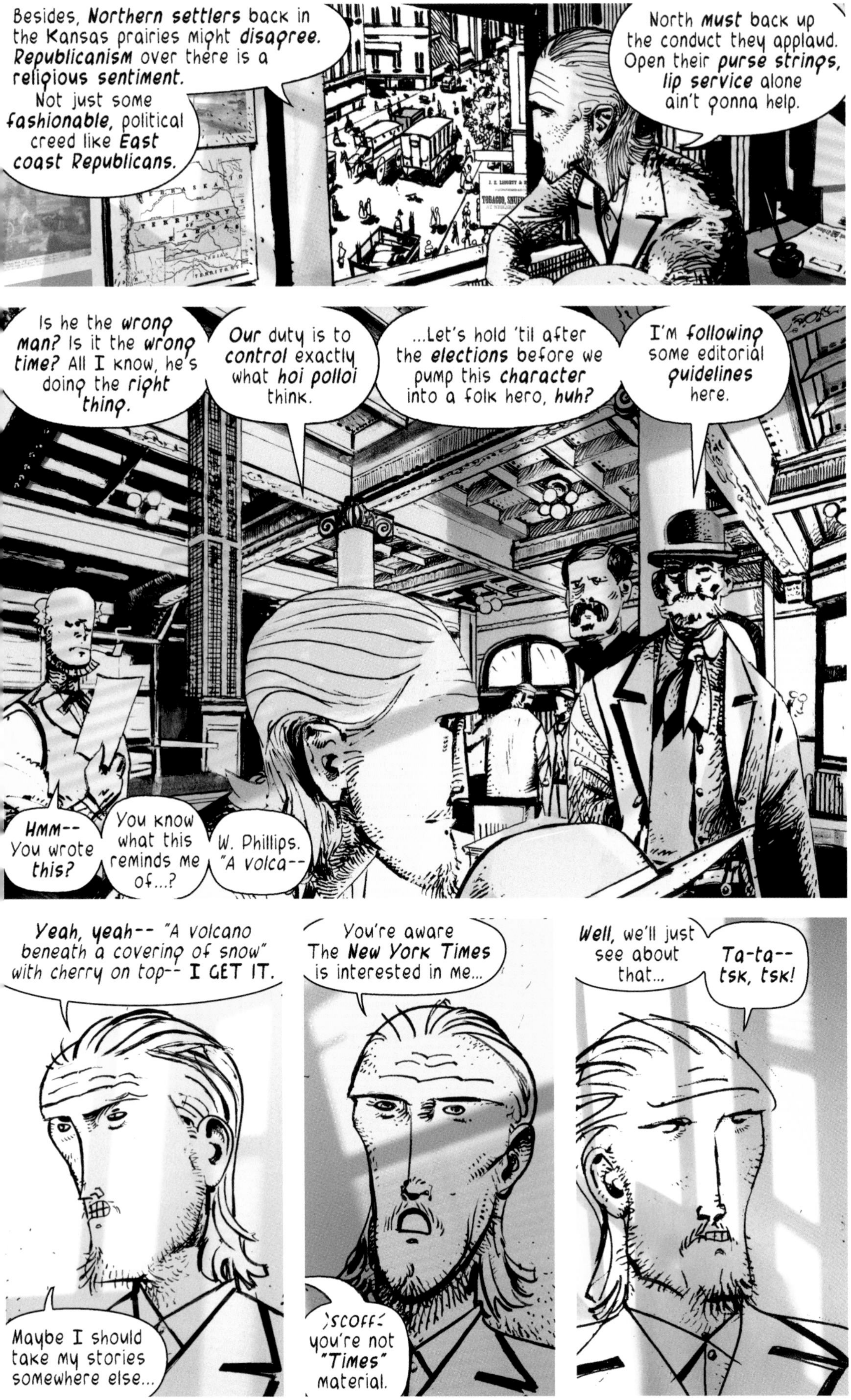

Besides, Northern settlers back in the Kansas prairies might disagree. Republicanism over there is a religious sentiment.
Not just some fashionable, political creed like East coast Republicans.
North must back up the conduct they applaud. Open their purse strings, lip service alone ain't gonna help.
Is he the wrong man? Is it the wrong time? All I know, he's doing the right thing.
Our duty is to control exactly what hoi polloi think.
...Let's hold 'til after the elections before we pump this character into a folk hero, huh?
I'm following some editorial guidelines here.
HMM-- You wrote this?
You know what this reminds me of...?
W. Phillips. "A volca--
Yeah, yeah-- "A volcano beneath a covering of snow" with cherry on top-- I GET IT.
Maybe I should take my stories somewhere else...
You're aware The New York Times is interested in me...
SCOFF you're not "Times" material.
Well, we'll just see about that...
Ta-ta-- tsk, tsk!

There is no fear of God before their eyes

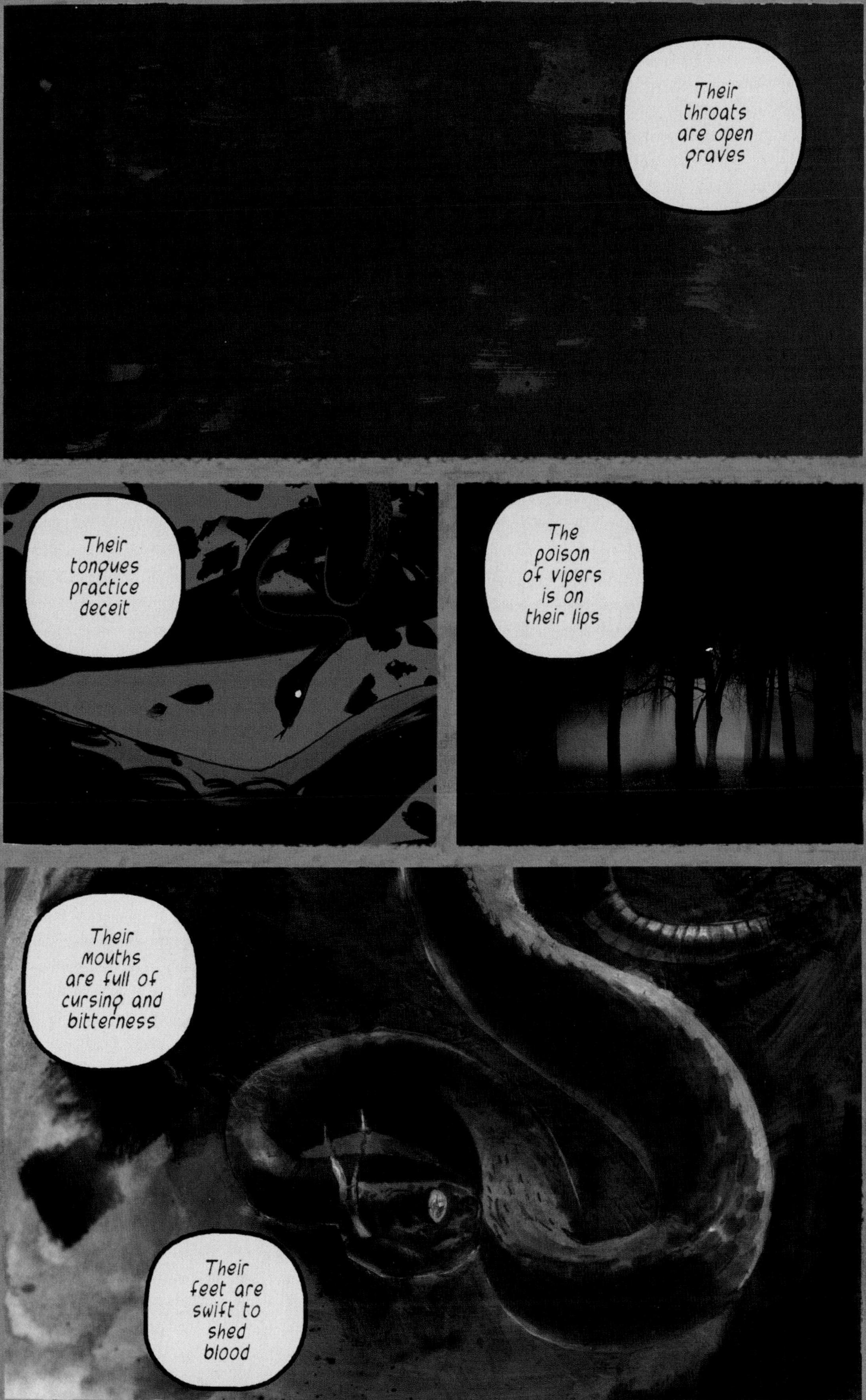
Their throats are open graves
Their tongues practice deceit
The poison of vipers is on their lips
Their mouths are full of cursing and bitterness
Their feet are swift to shed blood

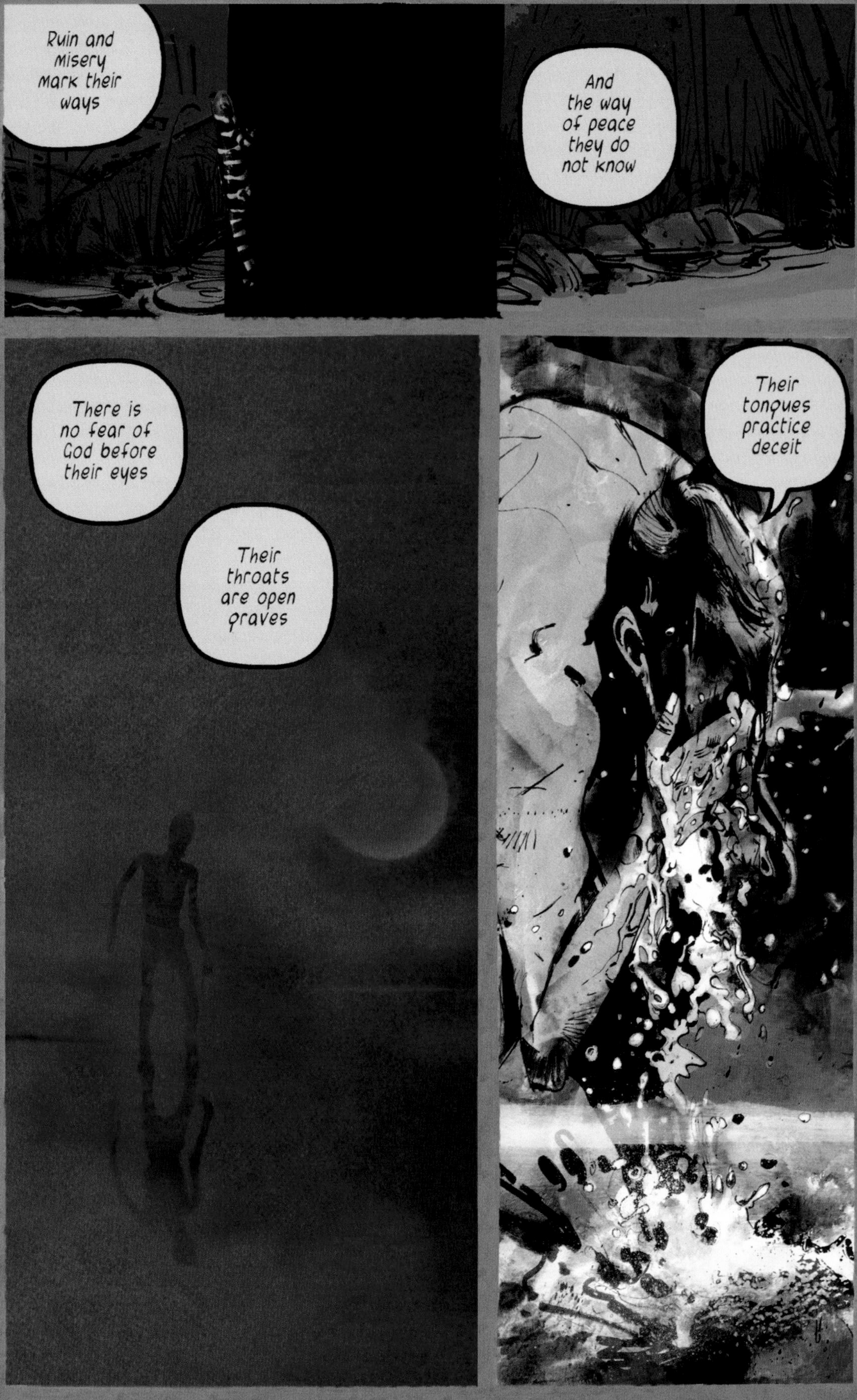
Ruin and misery mark their ways
And the way of peace they do not know
There is no fear of God before their eyes
Their throats are open graves
Their tongues practice deceit

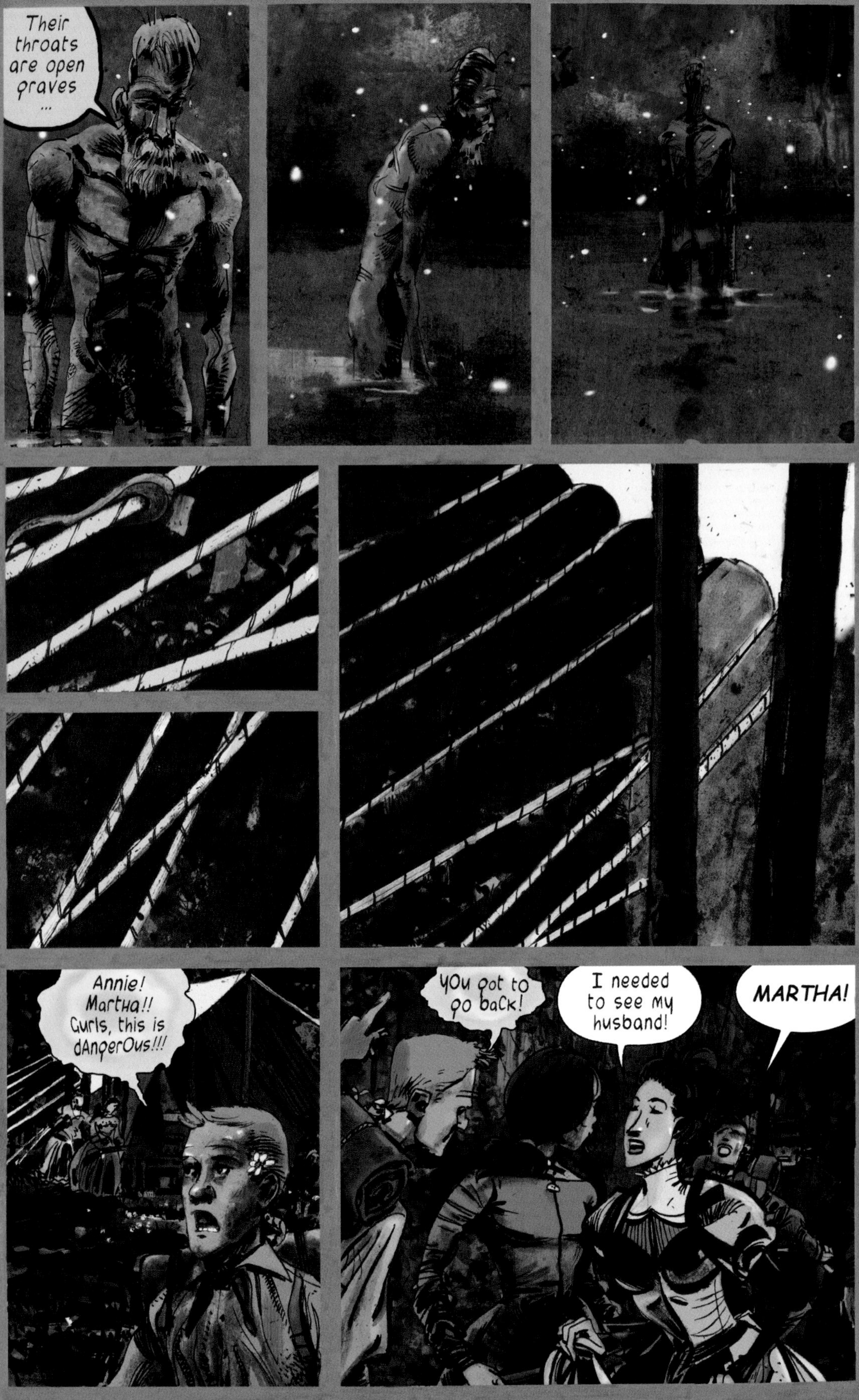
Their throats are open graves ...
Annie! Martha!! Gurls, this is dAngerOus!!!
yOu got to go bAck!
I needed to see my husband!
MARTHA!

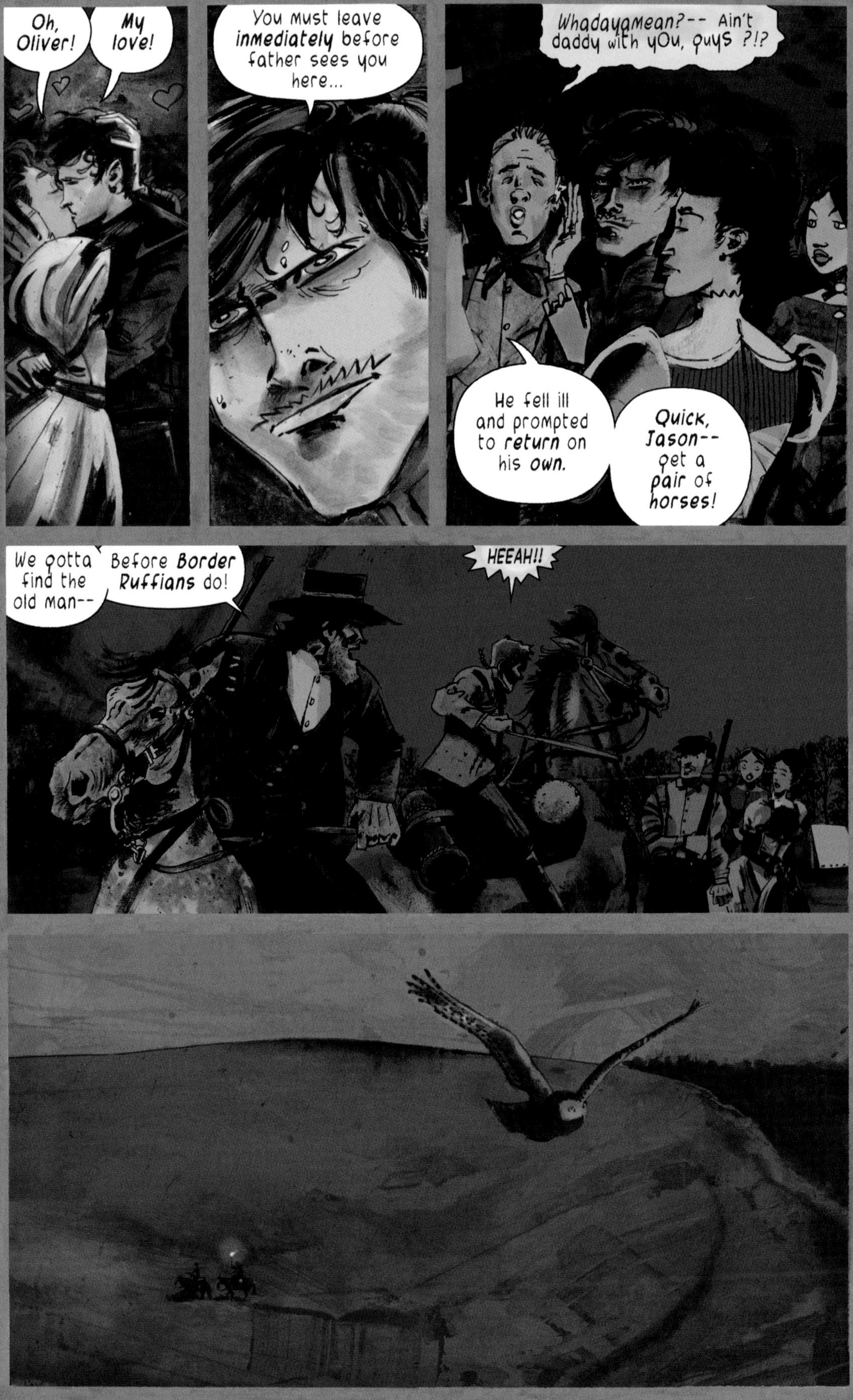

Oh, Oliver!
My love!
You must leave immediately before father sees you here...
Whadayamean?-- Ain't daddy with you, guys ?!?
He fell ill and prompted to return on his own.
Quick, Jason-- get a pair of horses!
We gotta find the old man--
Before Border Ruffians do!
HEEAH!!

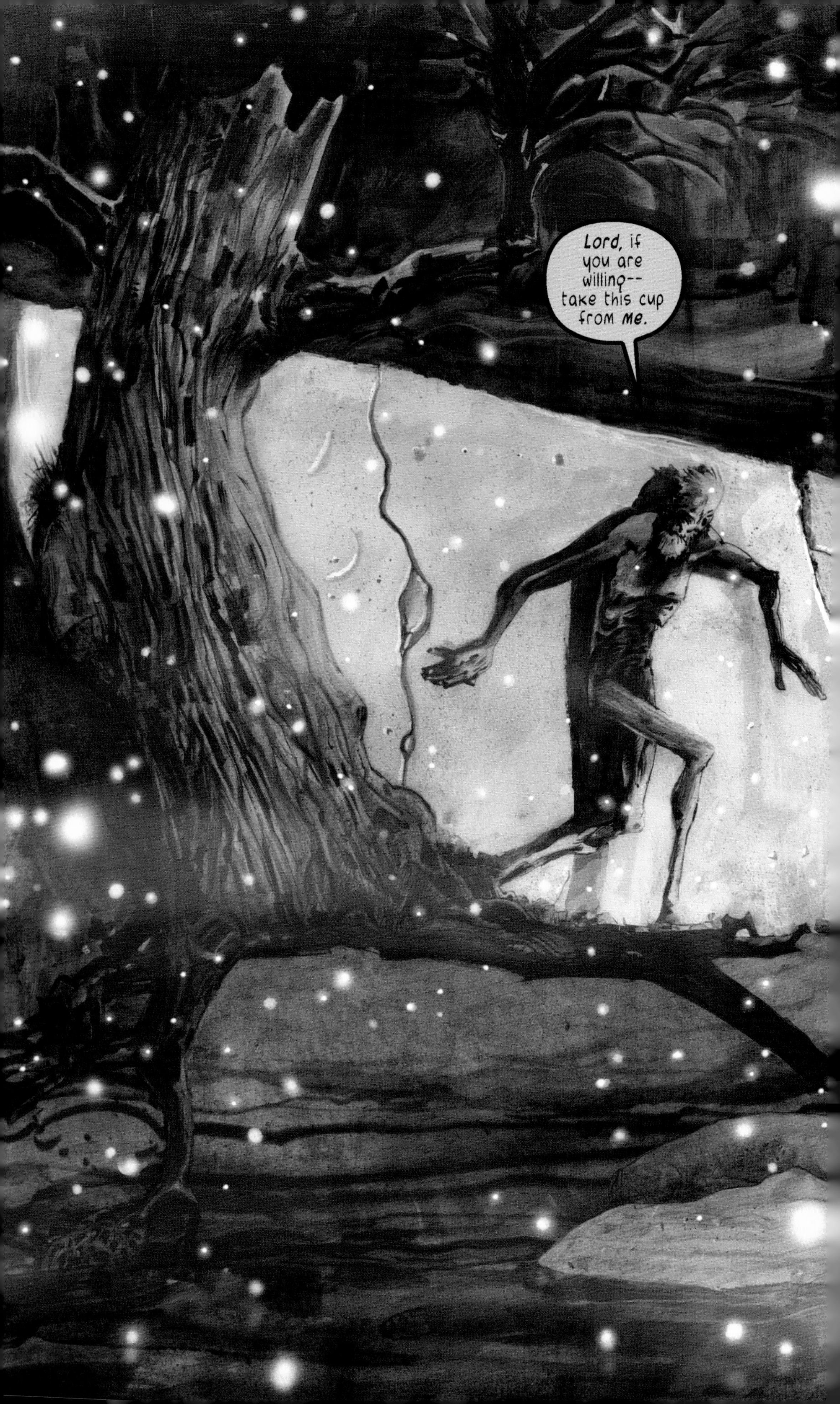
Lord, if you are willing-- take this cup from me.

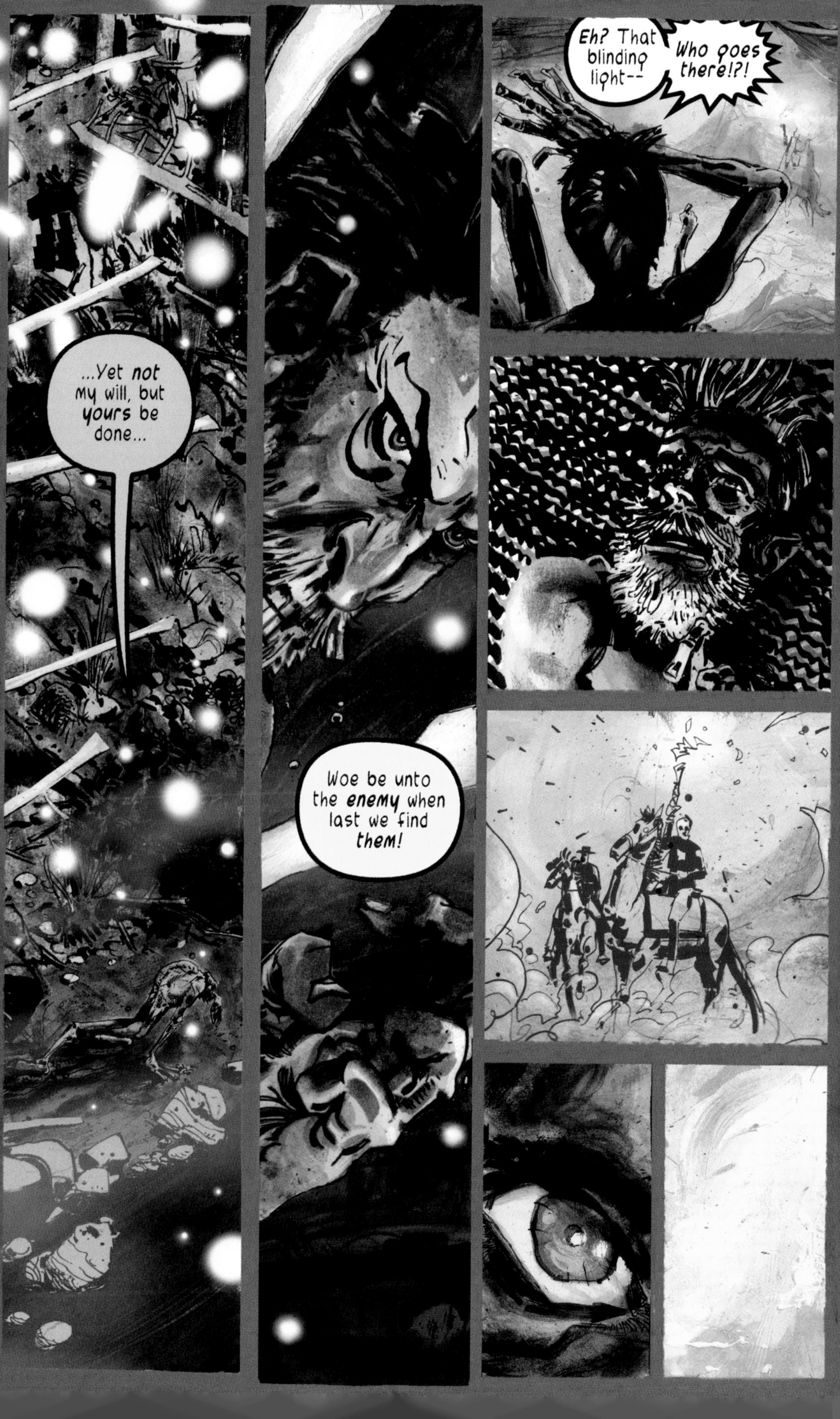
...Yet not my will, but yours be done...
Woe be unto the enemy when last we find them!
Eh? That blinding light--
Who goes there!?!

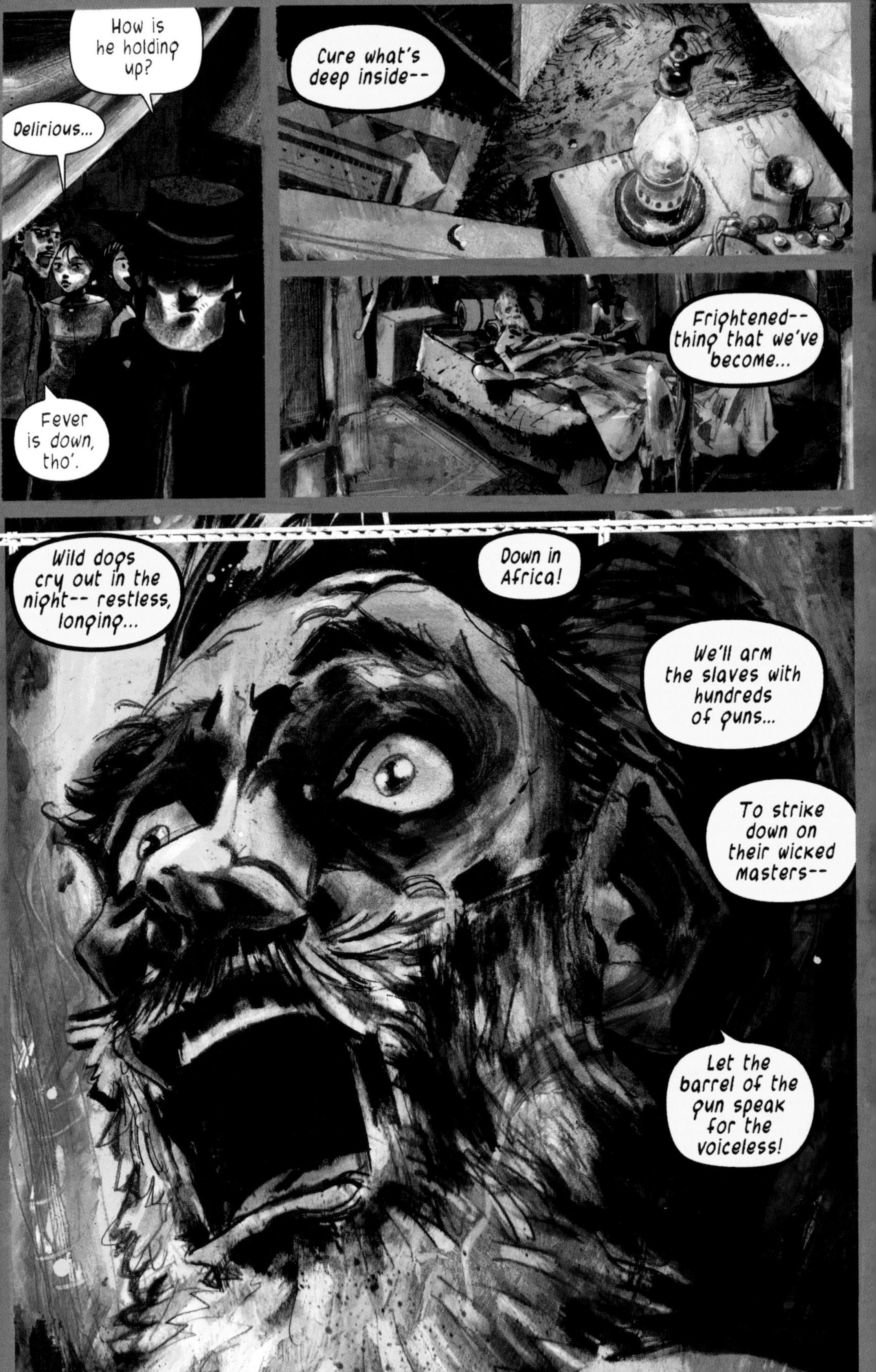
How is he holding up?
Delirious...
Fever is down, tho'.
Cure what's deep inside--
Frightened--thing that we've become...
Wild dogs cry out in the night-- restless, longing...
Down in Africa!
We'll arm the slaves with hundreds of guns...
To strike down on their wicked masters--
Let the barrel of the gun speak for the voiceless!

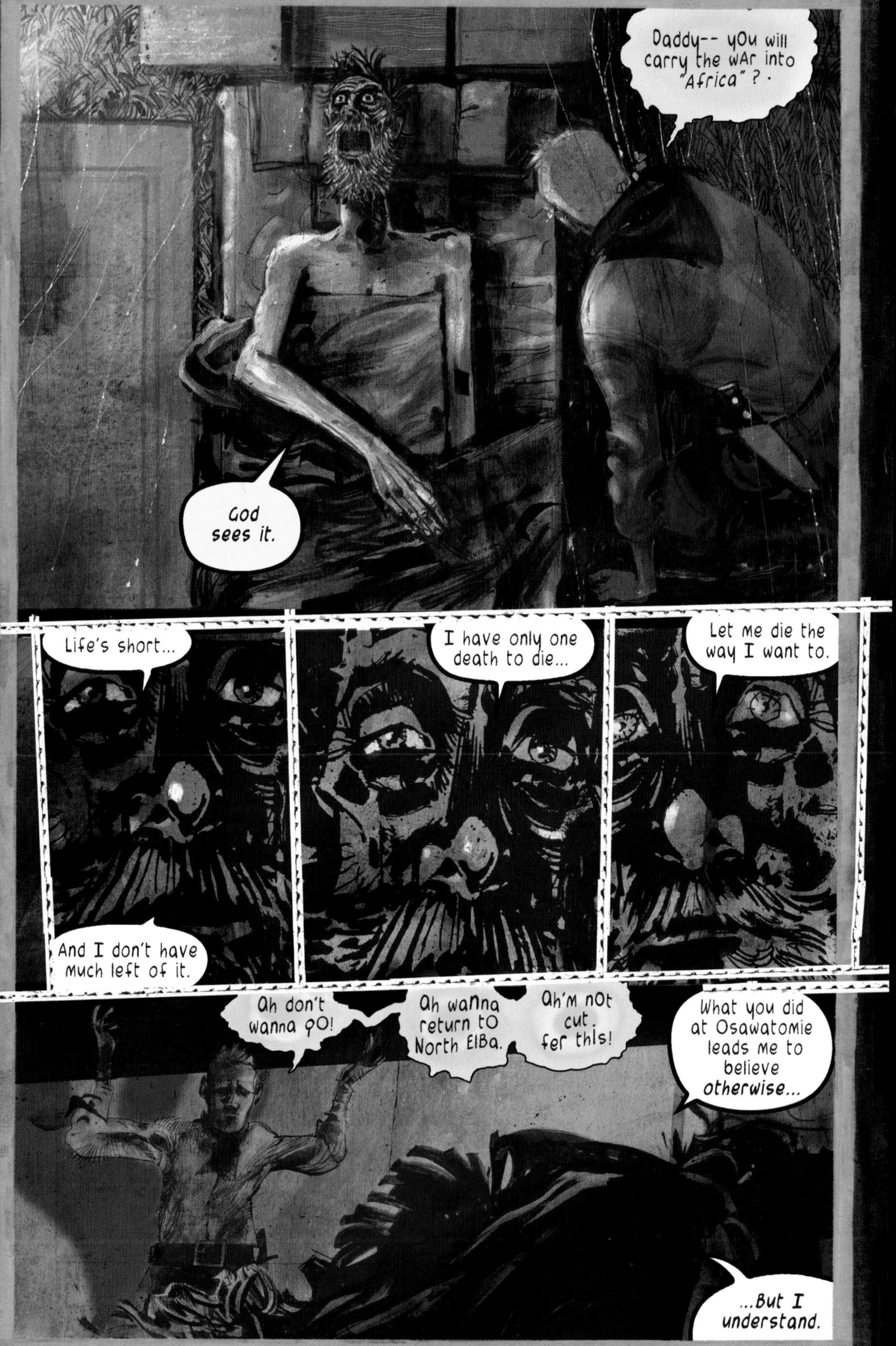
Daddy-- you will carry the war into "Africa"?
God sees it.
Life's short...
And I don't have much left of it.
I have only one death to die...
Let me die the way I want to.
Ah don't wanna go!
Ah wanna return to North Elba.
Ah'm not cut fer this!
What you did at Osawatomie leads me to believe *otherwise*...
...But I understand.

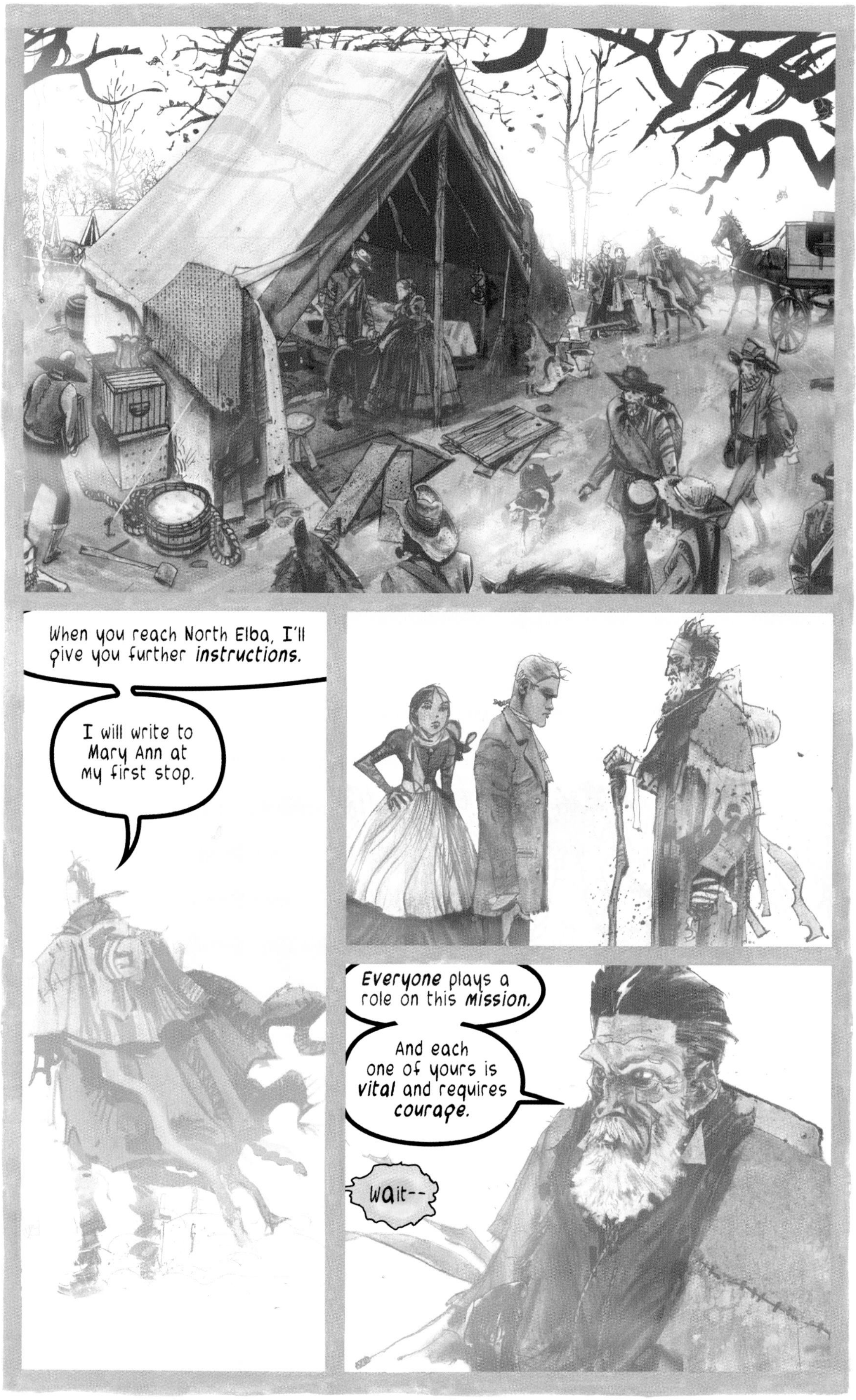
When you reach North Elba, I'll give you further *instructions.*
I will write to Mary Ann at my first stop.
Everyone plays a role on this *mission.*
And each one of yours is *vital* and requires *courage.*
Wait--

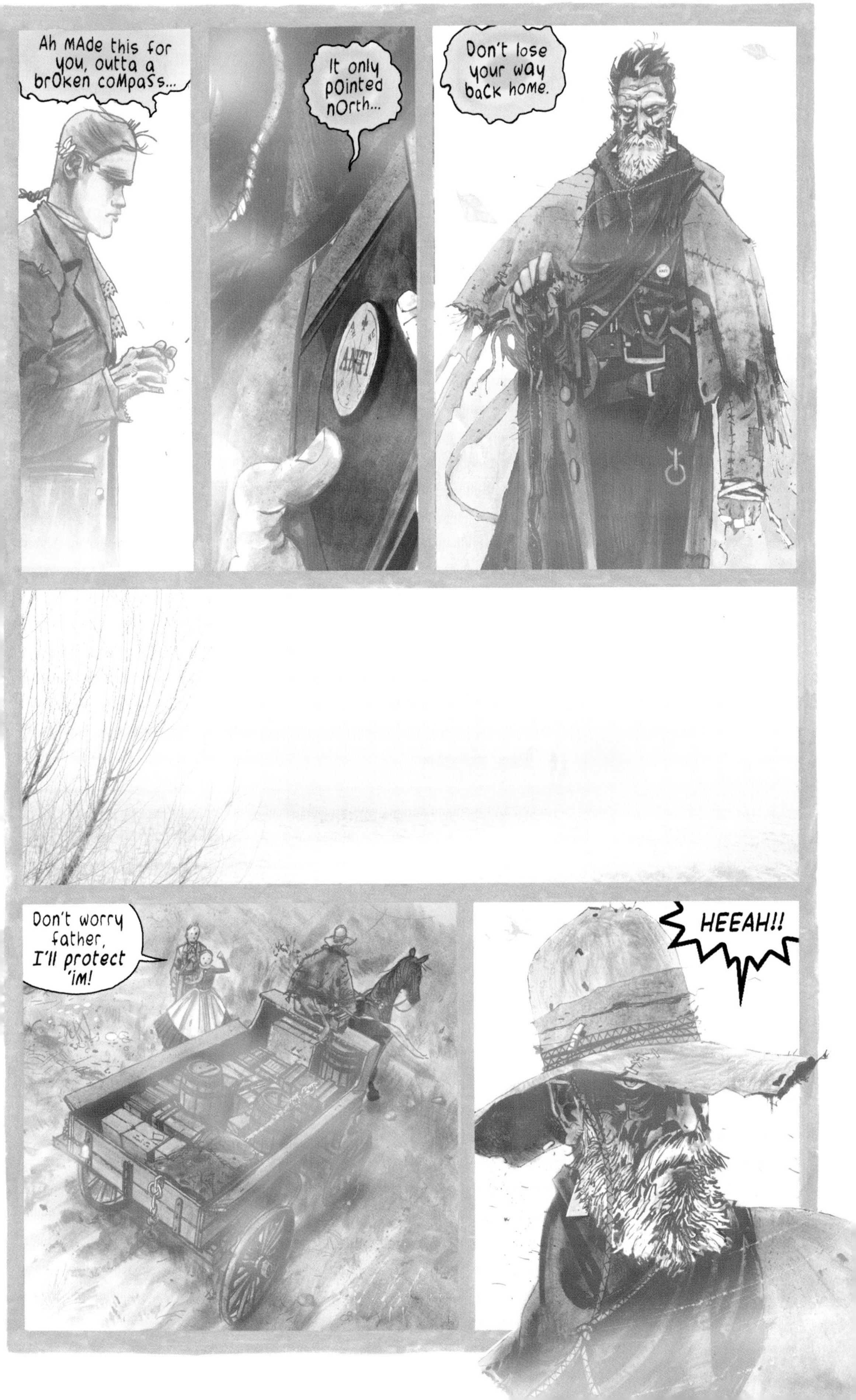
Ah MAde this for you, outta a brOken coMpaSs...
It only pOinted nOrth...
Don't lose your way back home.
Don't worry father, I'll protect 'im!
HEEAH!!

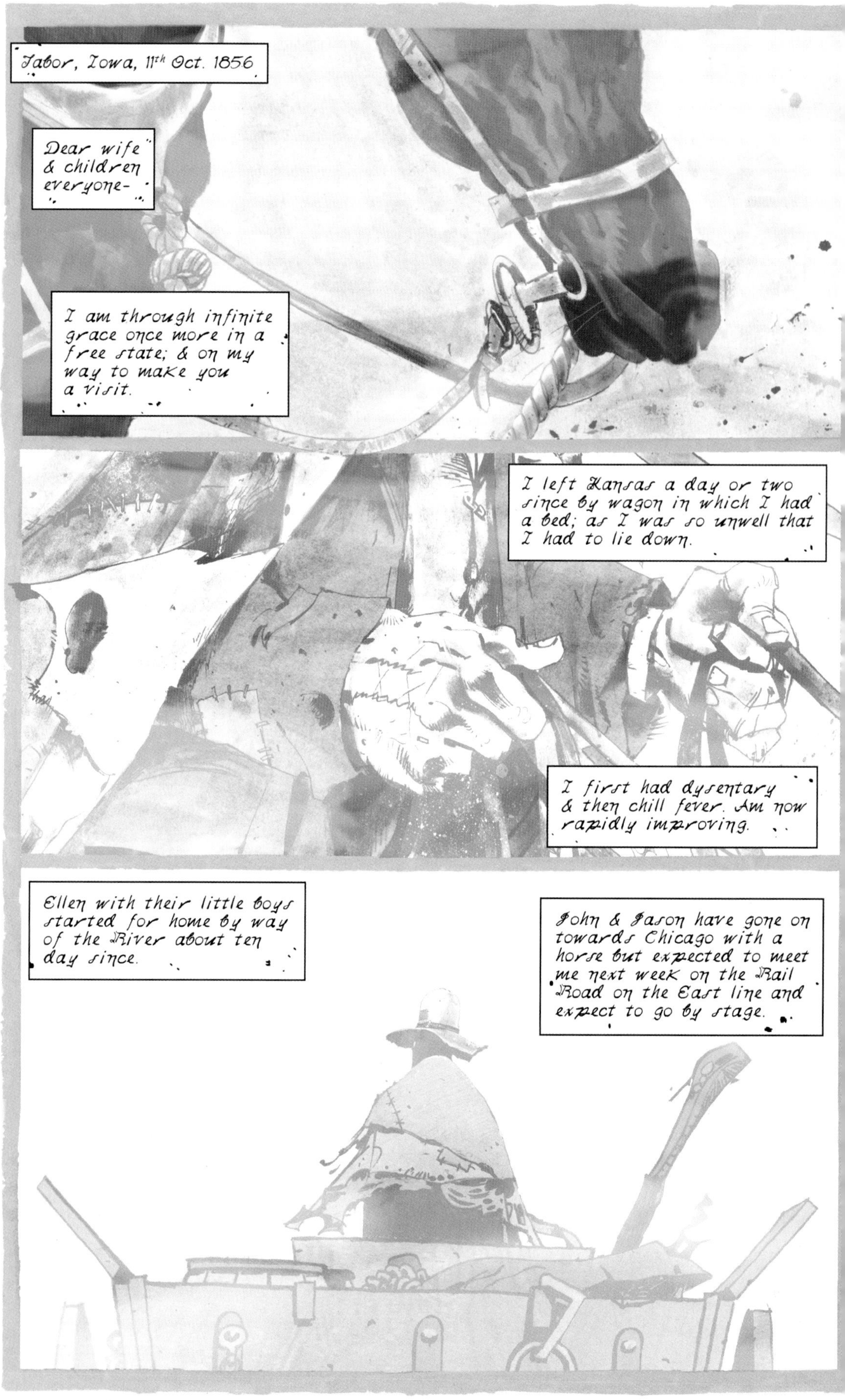
Tabor, Iowa, 11th Oct. 1856
Dear wife & children everyone-
I am through infinite grace once more in a free state; & on my way to make you a visit.
I left Kansas a day or two since by wagon in which I had a bed; as I was so unwell that I had to lie down.
I first had dysentary & then chill fever. Am now rapidly improving.
Ellen with their little boys started for home by way of the River about ten day since.
John & Jason have gone on towards Chicago with a horse but expected to meet me next week on the Rail Road on the East line and expect to go by stage.

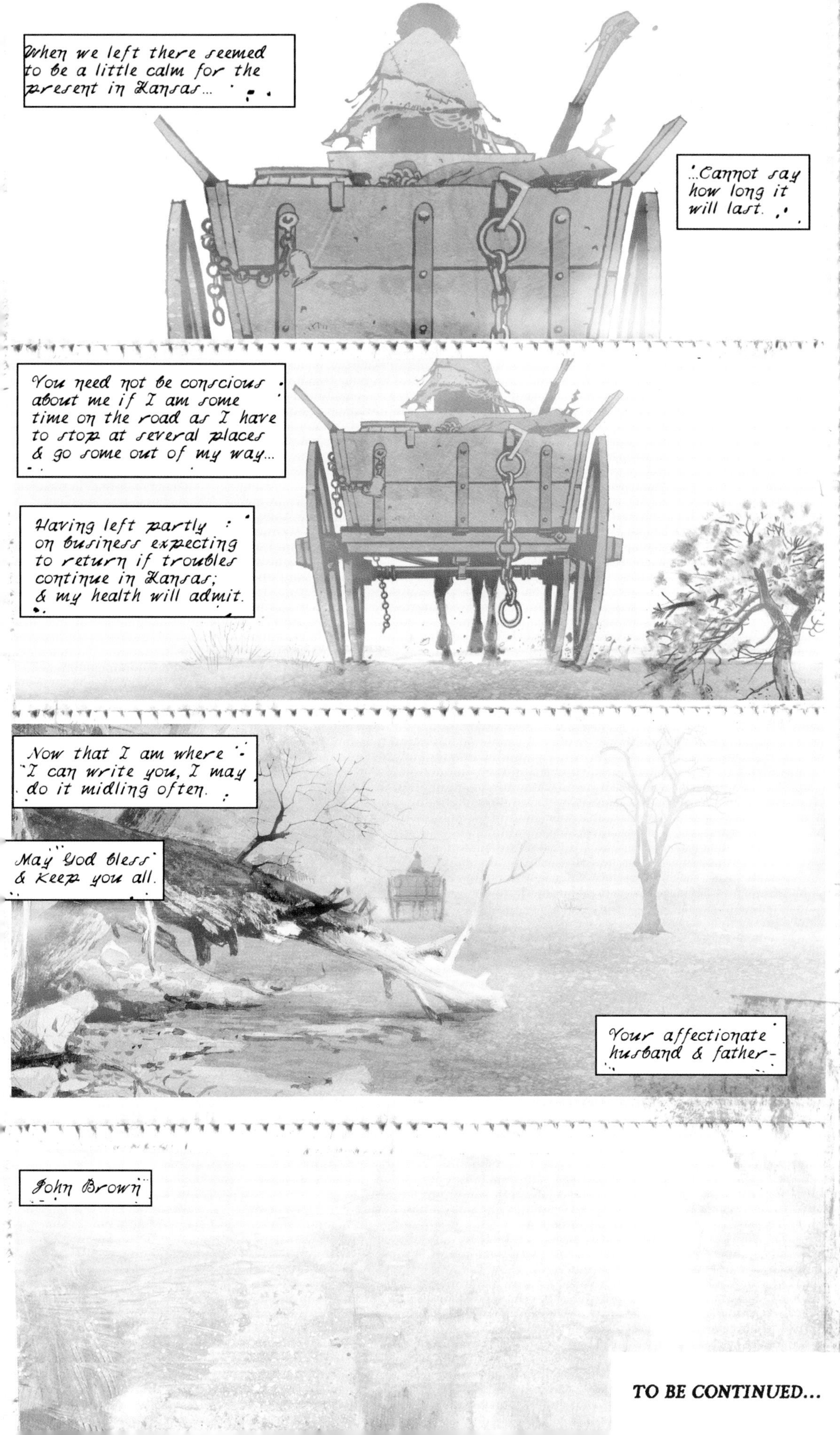
When we left there seemed to be a little calm for the present in Kansas...
...Cannot say how long it will last.
You need not be conscious about me if I am some time on the road as I have to stop at several places & go some out of my way...
Having left partly on business expecting to return if troubles continue in Kansas; & my health will admit.
Now that I am where I can write you, I may do it midling often.
May God bless & keep you all.
Your affectionate husband & father-
John Brown
TO BE CONTINUED...

Next On

THUNDERBOLT
AN AMERICAN TALE VOL. 2

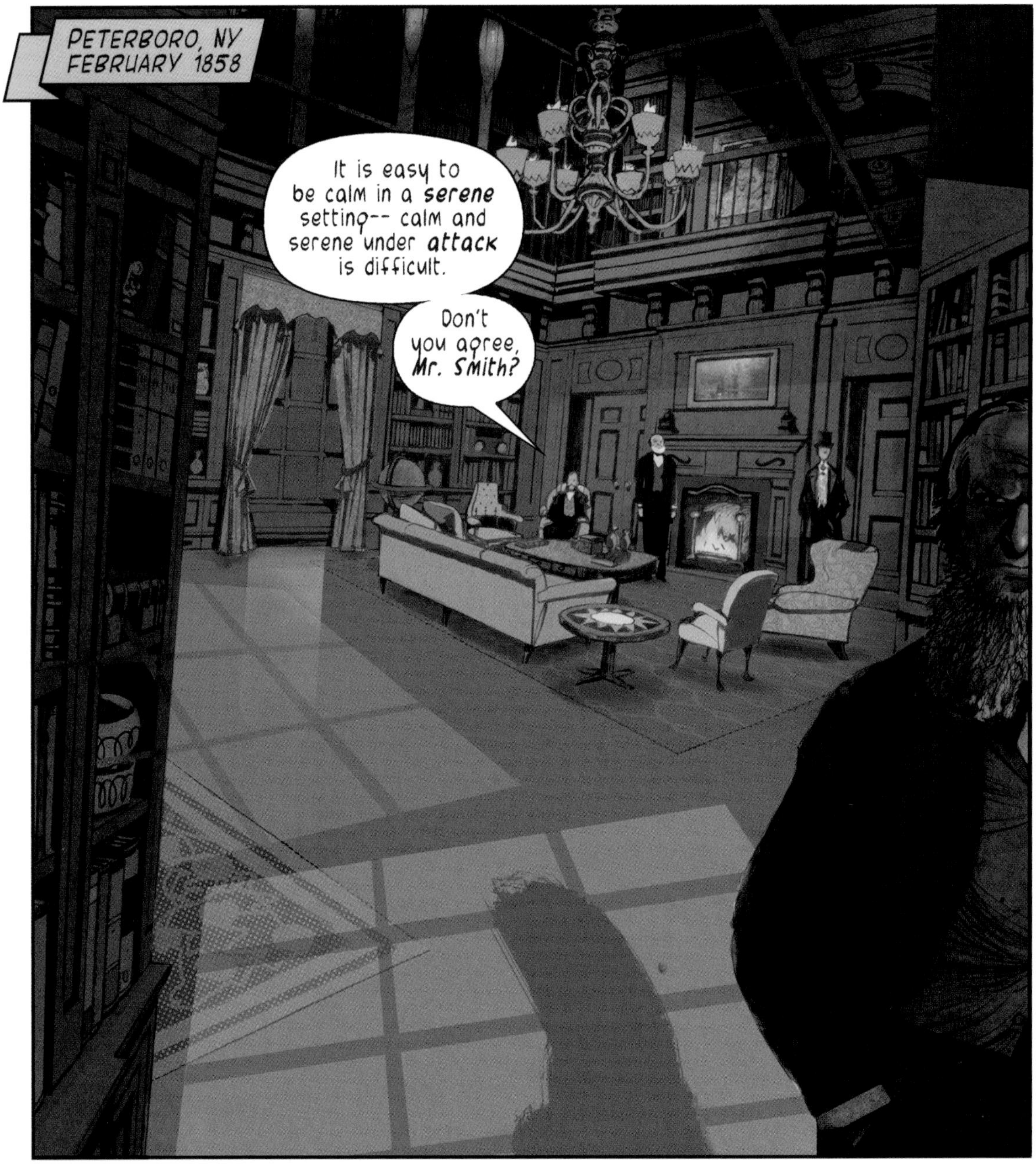
PETERBORO, NY
FEBRUARY 1858
It is easy to be calm in a serene setting-- calm and serene under attack is difficult.
Don't you agree, Mr. Smith?

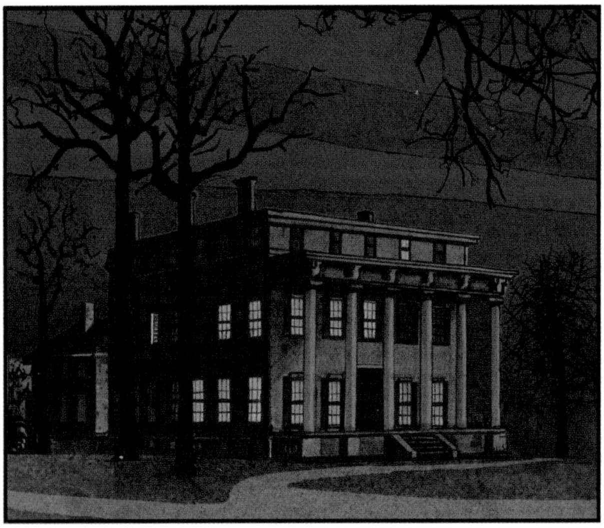

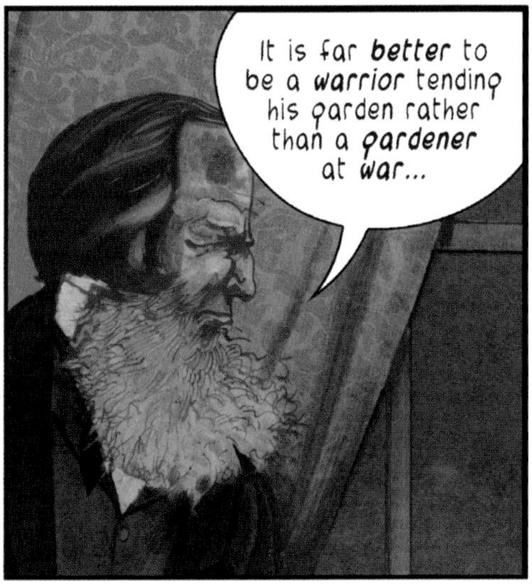
It is far better to be a warrior tending his garden rather than a gardener at war...

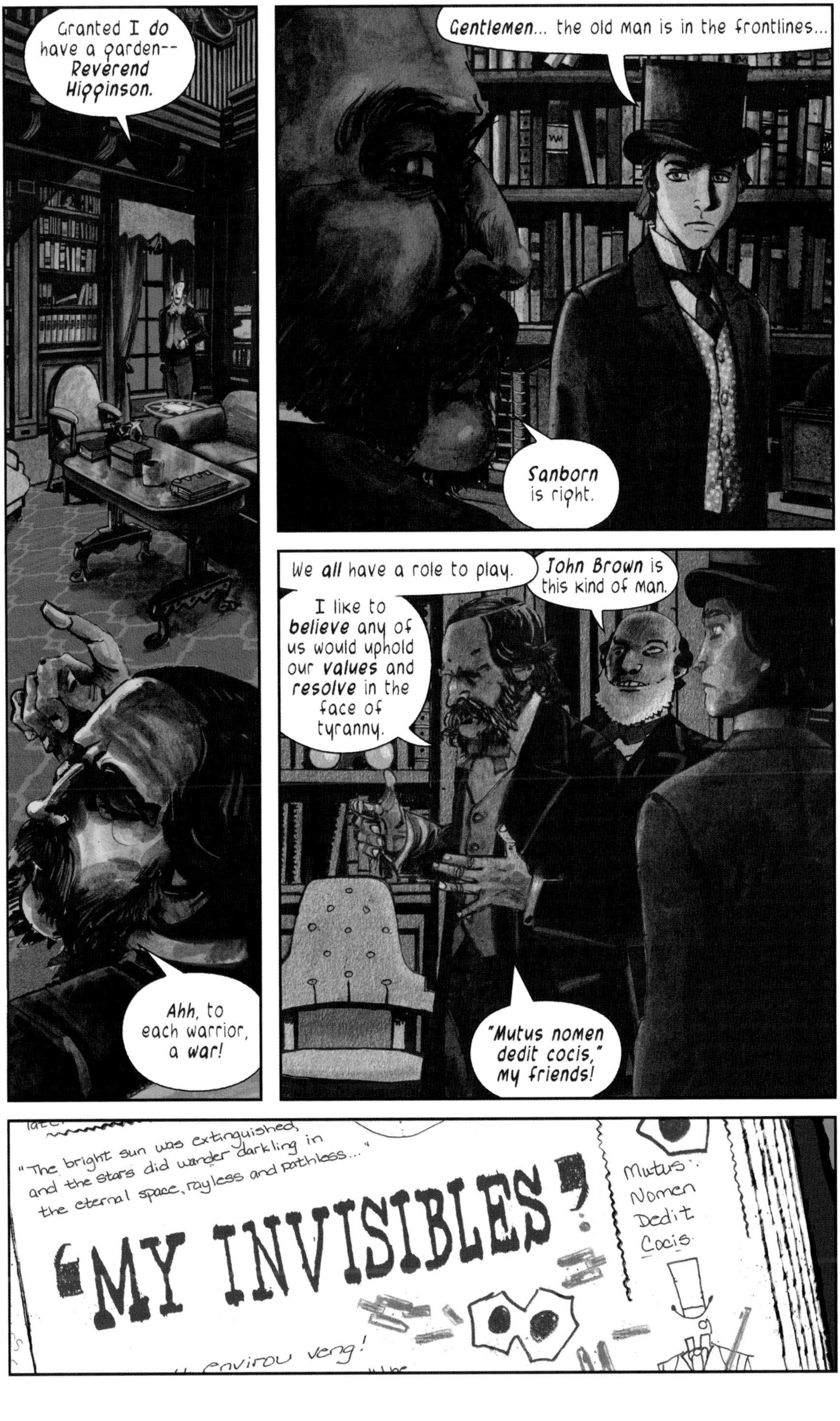
Granted I do have a garden-- Reverend Higginson.
Ahh, to each warrior, a war!
Gentlemen... the old man is in the frontlines...
Sanborn is right.
We all have a role to play.
I like to believe any of us would uphold our values and resolve in the face of tyranny.
John Brown is this kind of man.
"Mutus nomen dedit cocis," my friends!
"The bright sun was extinguished, and the stars did wander darkling in the eternal space, rayless and pathless..."
'MY INVISIBLES'
Mutus Nomen Dedit Cocis

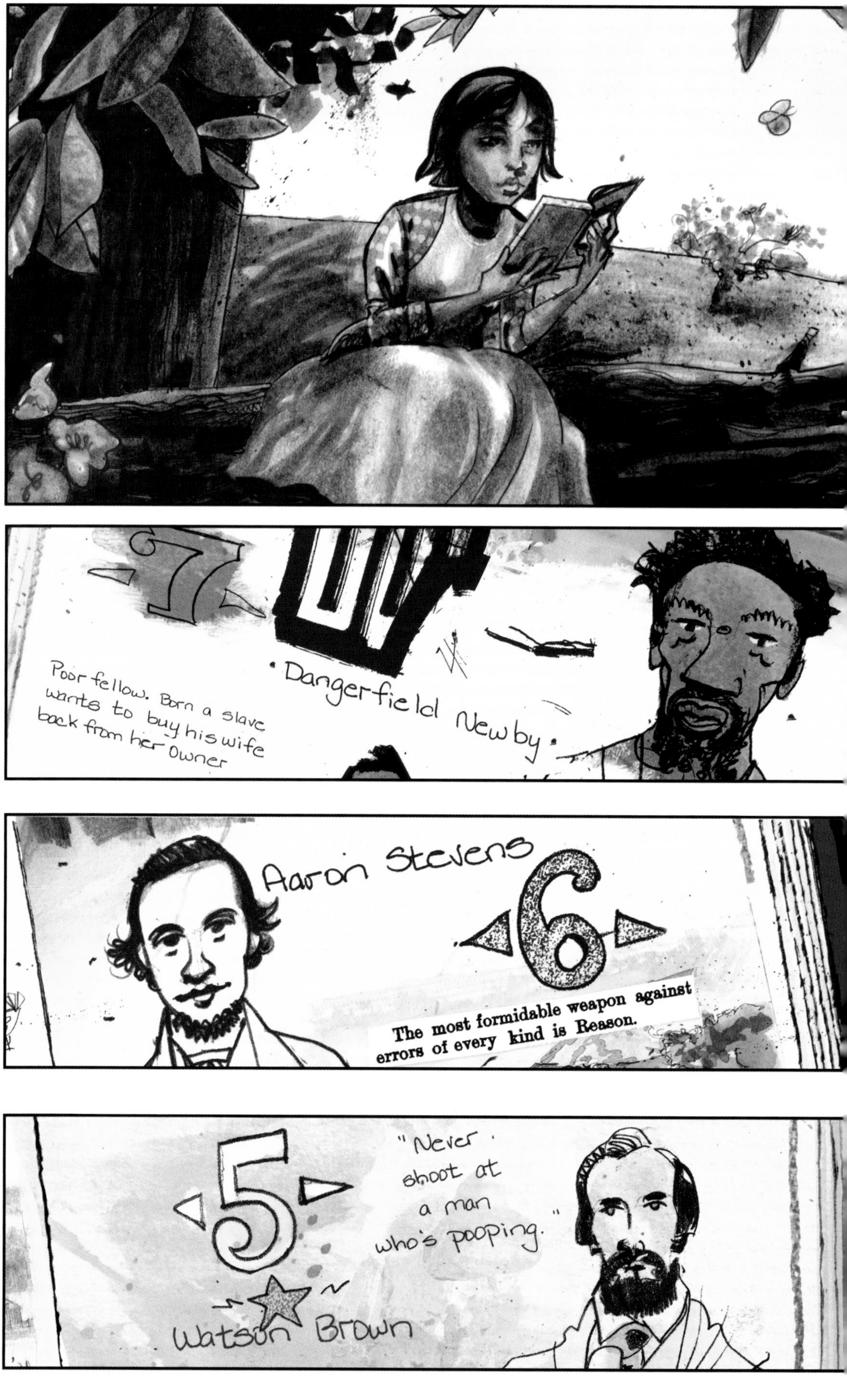
7
Dangerfield Newby
Poor fellow. Born a slave wants to buy his wife back from her owner
Aaron Stevens
6
The most formidable weapon against errors of every kind is Reason.
5
"Never shoot at a man who's pooping."
Watson Brown

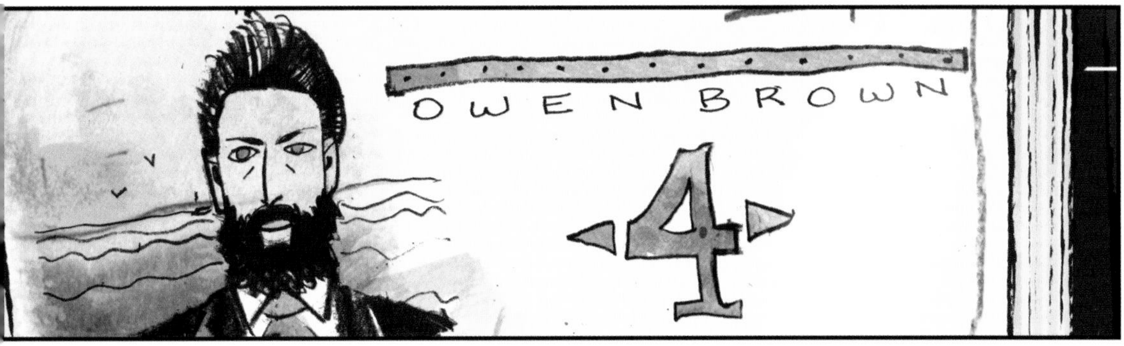
OWEN BROWN
4

Reconcile

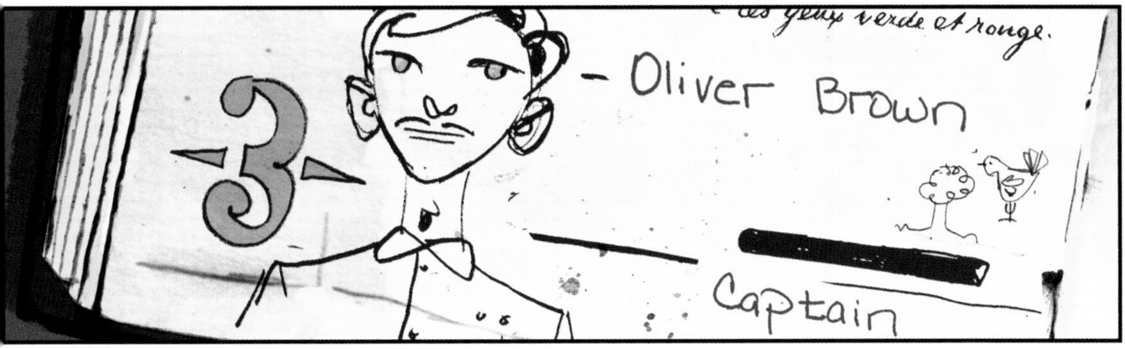
3
Oliver Brown
Captain

myself

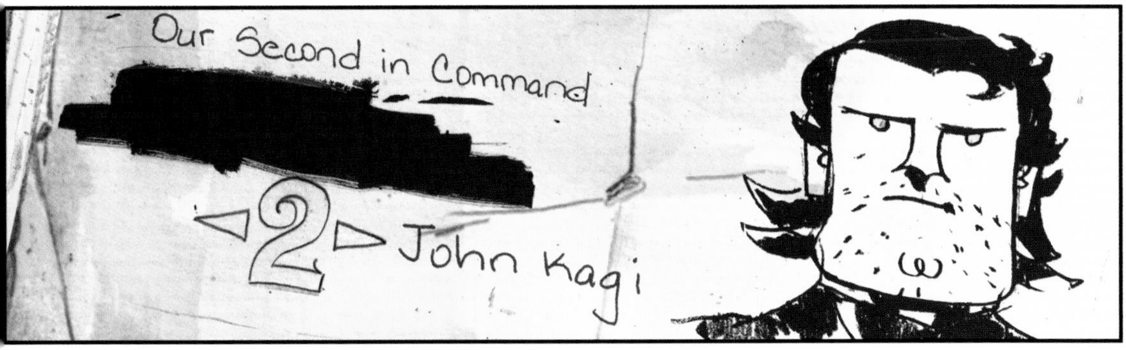
Our Second in Command
[redacted]
2
John Kagi

to this:

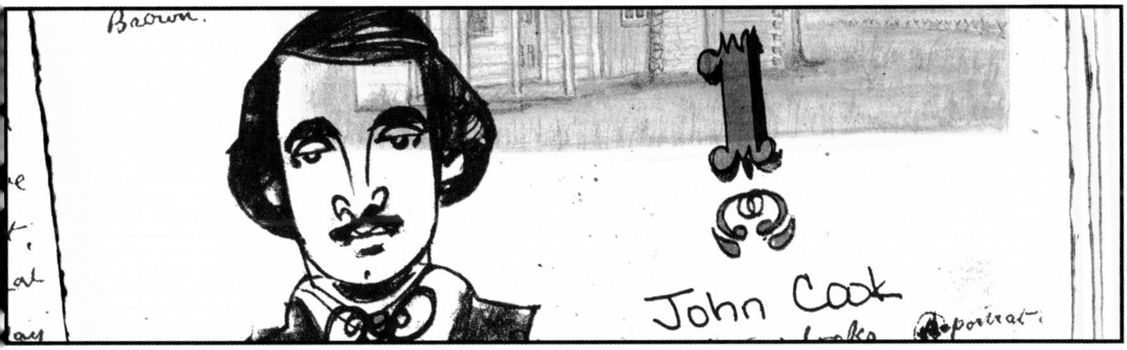
Brown.
1
John Cook

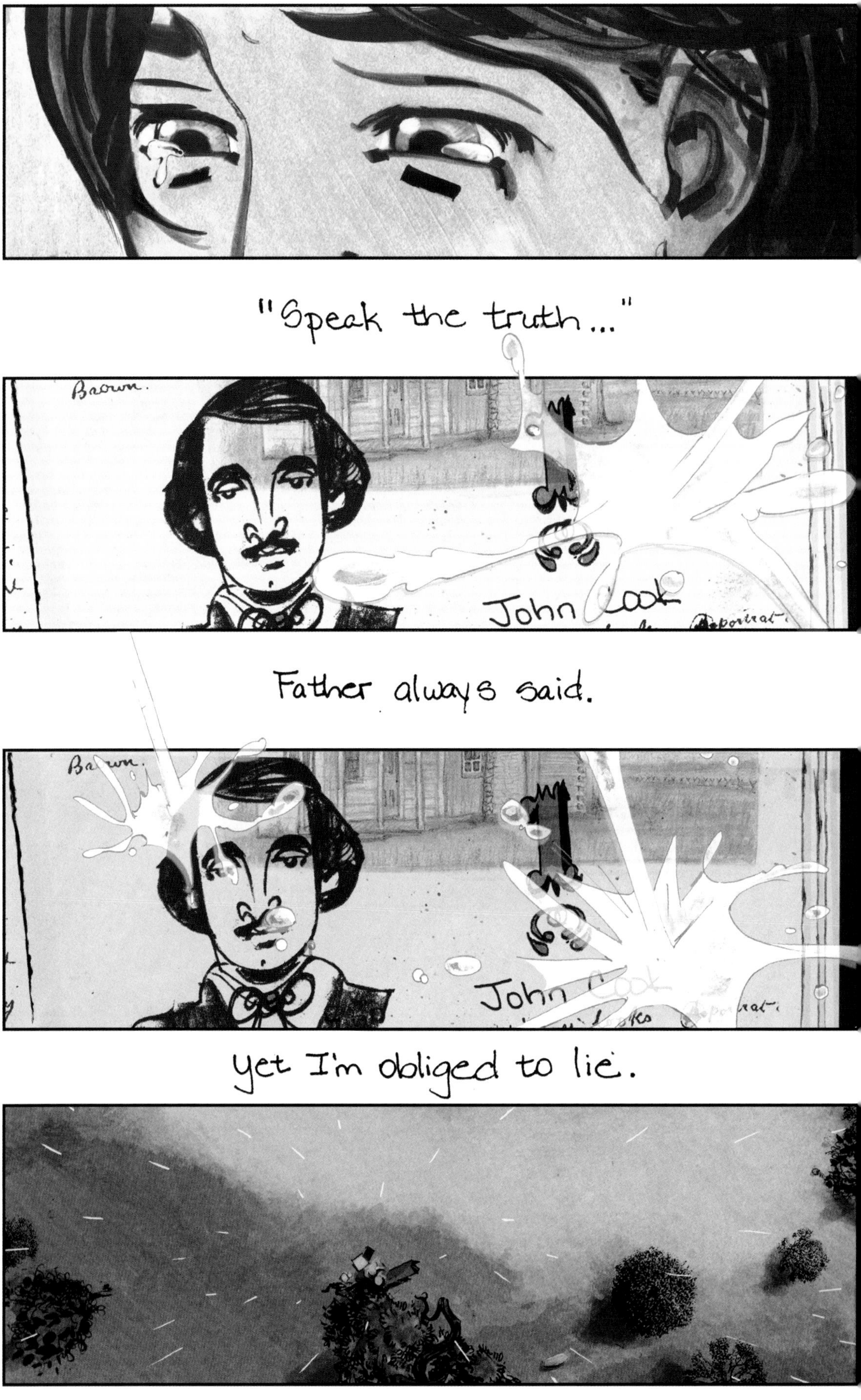
"Speak the truth..."
Brown.
John Cook
Father always said.
Brown.
John
yet I'm obliged to lie.

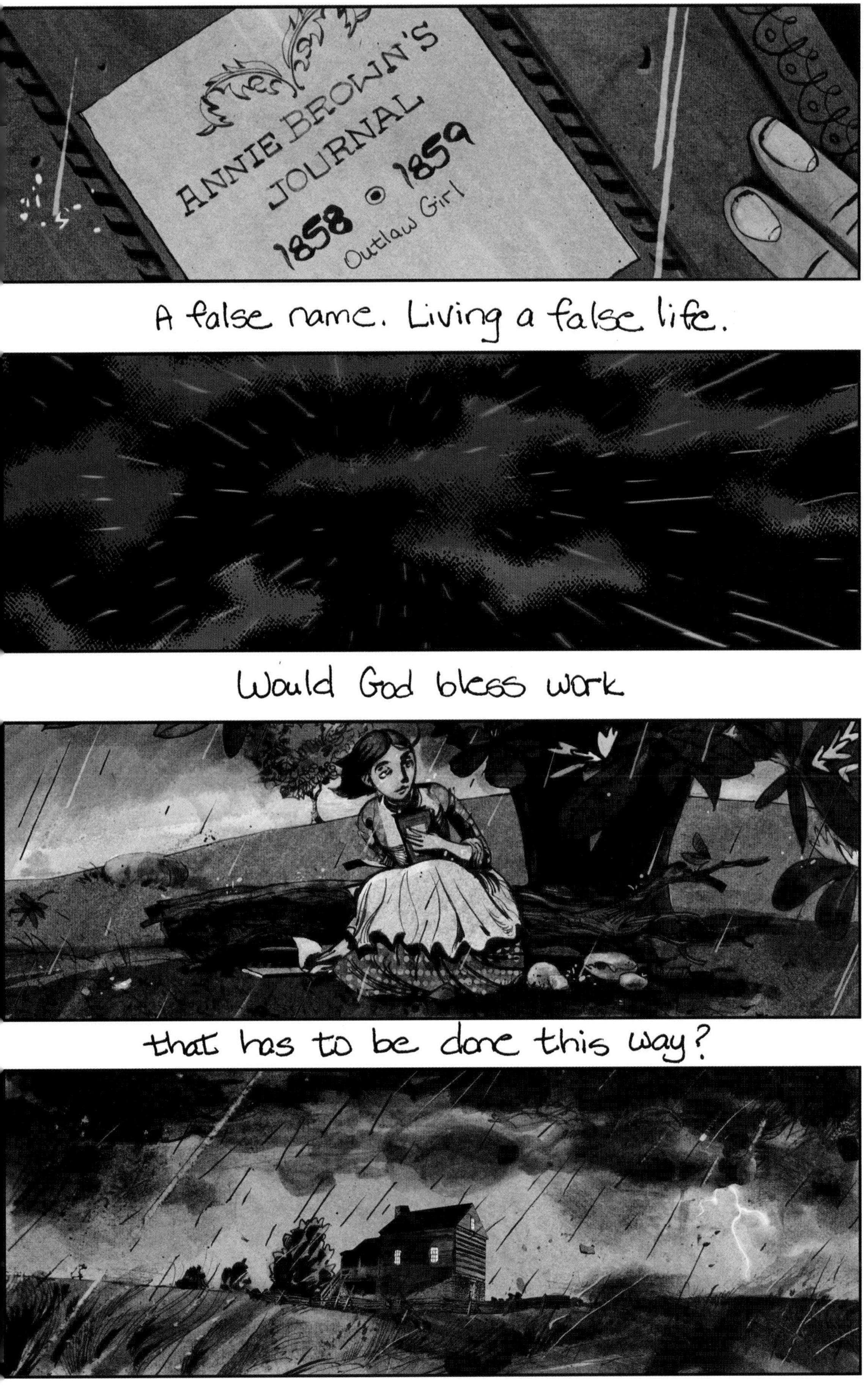

ANNIE BROWN'S
JOURNAL
1858 • 1859
Outlaw Girl
A false name. Living a false life.
Would God bless work
that has to be done this way?

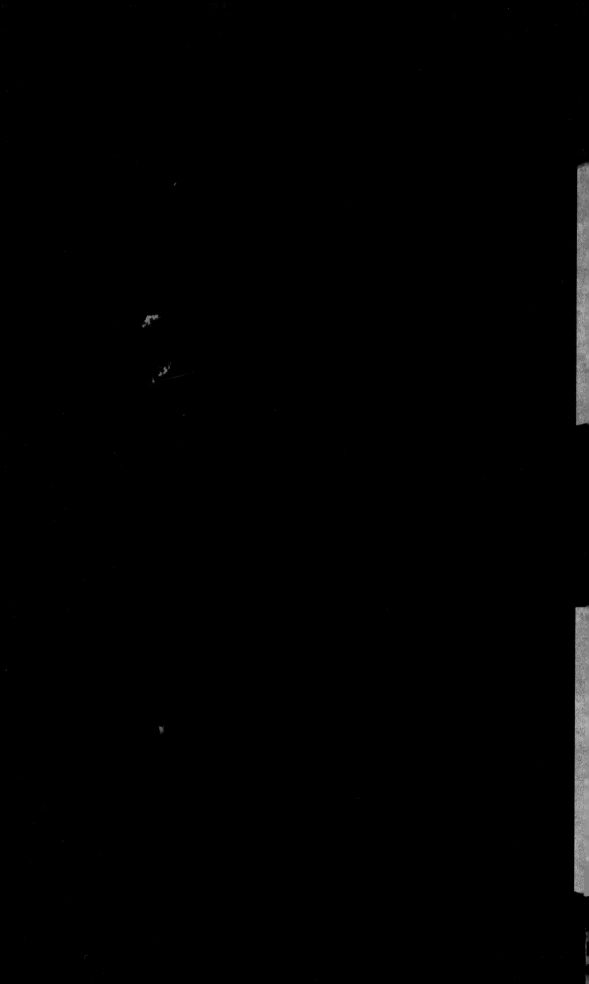

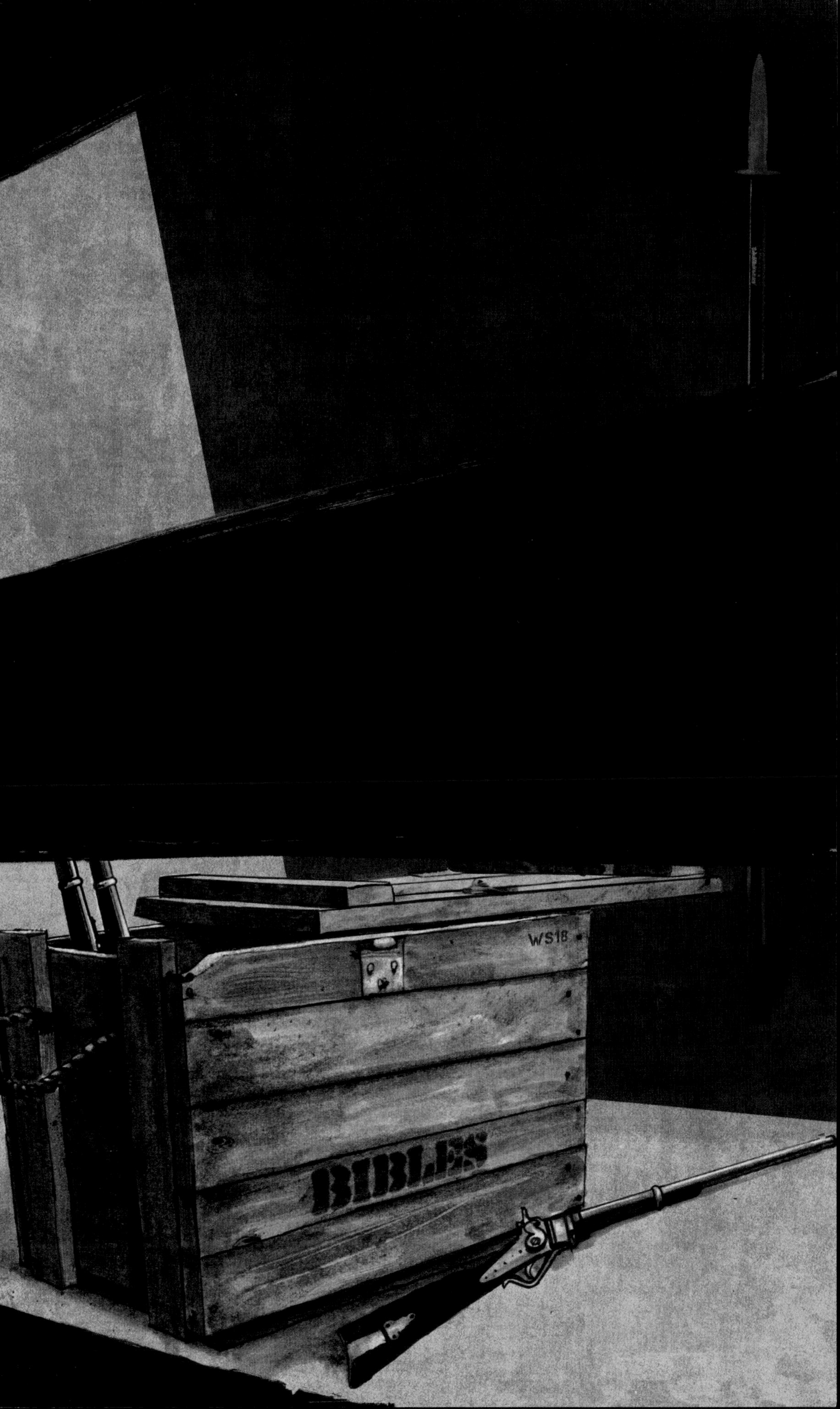
WS18
BIBLES

ACKNOWLEDGEMENTS

To Kristen Elias Rowley, Frederick Aldama, Geof Darrow, Edgar Allan Paz, Jim Morgensen, William Callahan, The Ohio State Press, Kansas Historical Society, the Perseus Digital Library Project, the Library of Congress, the NRA National Firearms Museum, Inkwell Management and Alex Cotto, thanks for your help, advice, and support.

Respect to Alex Toth, Moebiüs, Winslow Homer, Bill Sienkiewicz, John Buscema, Mike Mignola, and Sergio Toppi—bottomless sources of inspiration.

WS18

TO PHOENIX

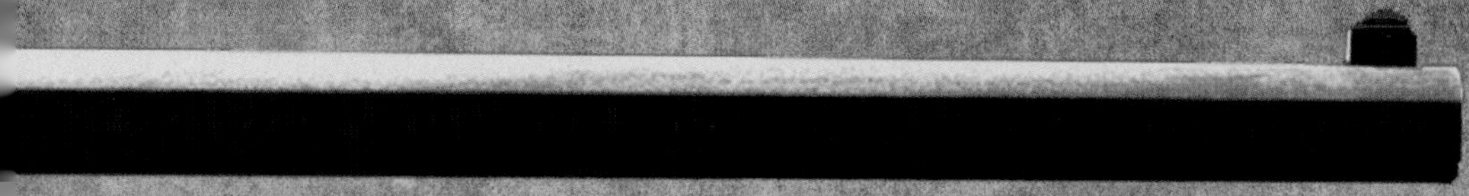

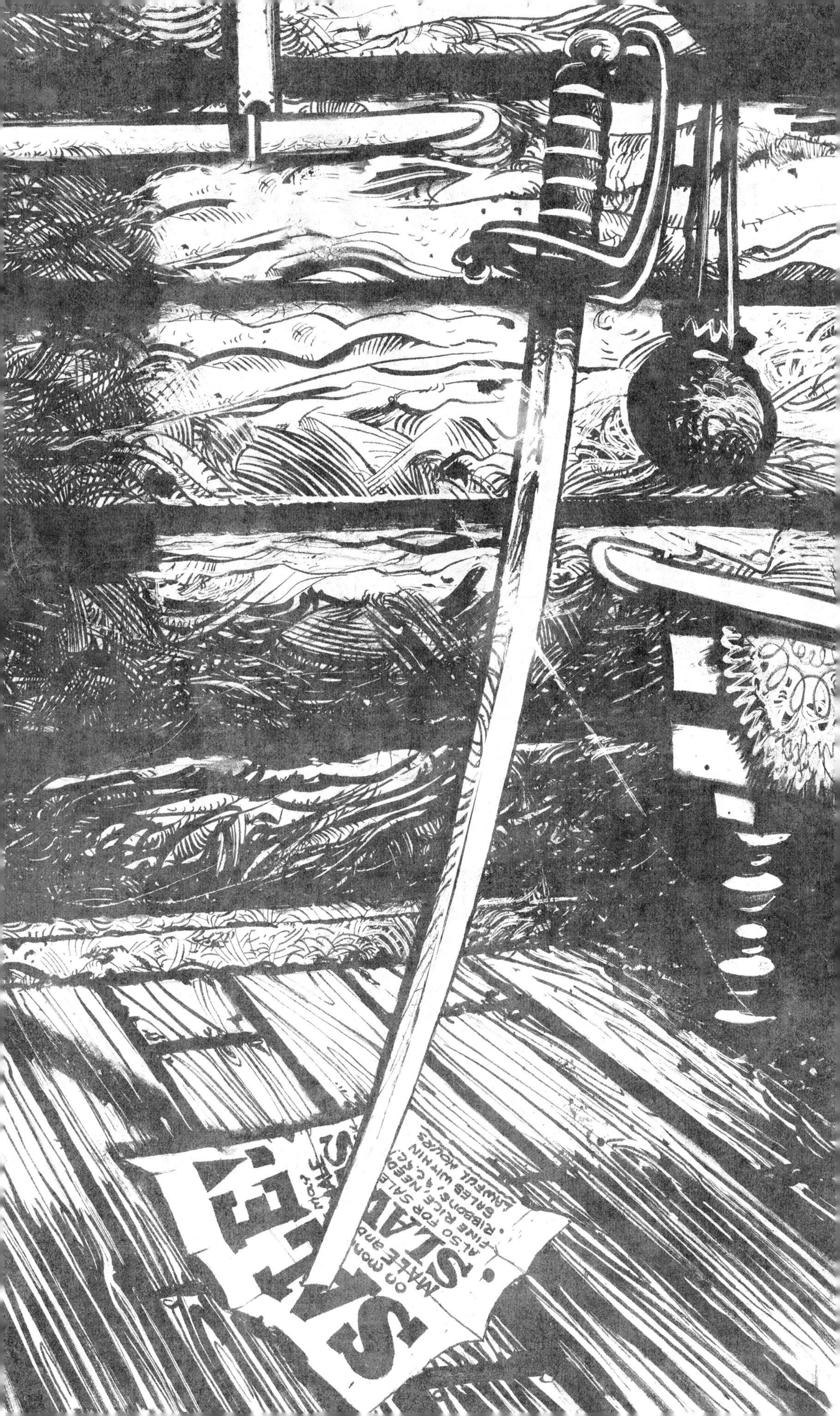
MALE and
ALSO FOR SALE
FINE RICE, NEEDLES,
RIBBONS, &C. &C.
SALES WITHIN
LAWFUL HOURS

THUNDERBOLT VOL.

AN AMERICAN TALE

WRITTEN & ILLUSTRATED BY WILFRED SANTIAGO

EDITED BY **SANLIDA CHENG**

BOOK DESIGN BY **WILFRED SANTIAGO**

SOUNDTRACK AVAILABLE AT **JOHNBROWNBOOK.COM**
MUSIC BY **DARIO ARGOSY**

THUNDERBOLT: AN AMERICAN TALE VOL. 1
Copyright © 2019 The Ohio State University.

SUMMARY • The true story of one of the most controversial figures
in American history, abolitionist John Brown. Dying is part of the plan.

Published by
MAD CREEK BOOKS
| USA |

An imprint of The Ohio State University Press
Columbus

WWW.OHIOSTATEPRESS.ORG

PRINTED IN KOREA

Library of Congress Cataloging-in-Publication data available online at catalog.loc.gov

FIRST EDITION 2019
ISBN: 978-0-8142-5548-3

10 9 8 7 6 5 4 3 2 1

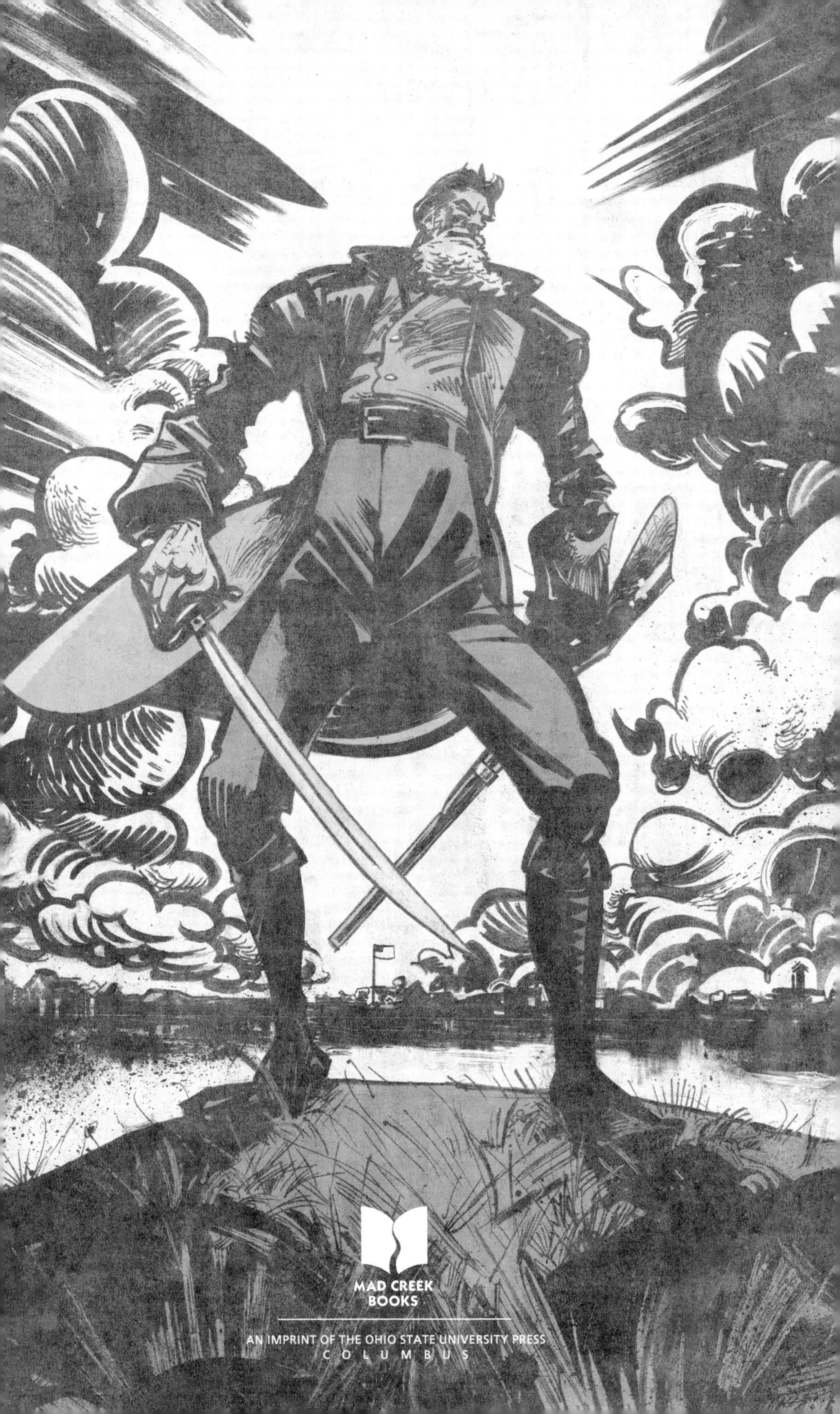

MAD CREEK BOOKS
AN IMPRINT OF THE OHIO STATE UNIVERSITY PRESS
COLUMBUS

OTHER BOOKS BY WILFRED SANTIAGO

MICHAEL
JORDAN
BULL ON PARADE
A GRAPHIC NOVEL BY WILFRED SANTIAGO

"21"
A GRAPHIC NOVEL by WILFRED SANTIAGO
THE STORY OF ROBERTO
CLEMENTE
21

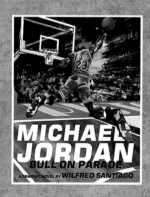

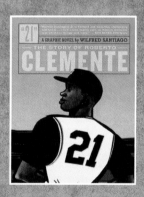

GOODWILFRED.COM

WILFRED SANTIAGO's

MICHAEL JORDAN: Bull on Parade is a *New York Times* bestseller and has been featured on ESPN and the *Chicago Tribune*, among others. The critically acclaimed biography *21: The Story of Roberto Clemente* was one of *Library Journal*'s 10 best graphic novels of 2011, featured in *Sports Illustrated* and nominated for a Casey Award. Santiago's work has been published by the *New York Times*, Marvel Comics, *Sports Illustrated*, Little, Brown Books, Dutton Books, DC Comics, and the *Chicago Tribune*. *THUNDERBOLT: An American Tale* is Santiago's fourth graphic novel. He lives somewhere in the midwest, among snakes, foxes, and coyotes.

Facts Notices.

THE BISON IS THE STATE ANIMAL OF KANSAS.

Bison is naturally leaner compared to beef. They are the largest indigenous animals native to North America. YUMMY!

LOCATION
LOCATION
LOCATION

Kansas' Smith County is the geographical center of the mainland. Dodge City Kansas is the windiest city in the United States. It's believed "KANSA" means *People of the south wind.*

'KANSA' were Native Americans who lived in what's now known as Kansas as early as 12,000 B.C.

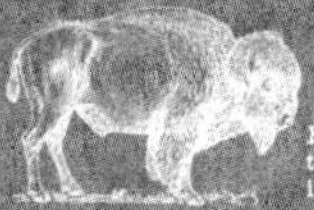

NEXT= THUNDERBOLT: An American Tale Volume 2

DRAWING ON ANGER
By Eric J. García

DRAWING ON ANGER
PORTRAITS OF U.S. HYPOCRISY
ERIC J. GARCÍA

MAD CREEK BOOKS

Mad Creek Books is the literary trade imprint of The Ohio State University Press.

DIARY OF A...
"POWERFUL"
PUBLISHERS WEEKLY
☆

DRAWING ON ANGER...
"GARCÍA SHEDS LIGHT"
JEN SORENSEN
☆

ANGELITOS...
"GRITTY"
THE NEW YORK TIMES
☆

TALES FROM LA VIDA...
"MIND BLOWING!"
KEITH KNIGHT

LATINOGRAPHIX
AVAILABLE WHERE
· BOOKS ARE SOLD ·

TALES FROM LA VIDA
Edited by Frederick Luis Aldama

TALES FROM LA VIDA
A LATINX COMICS ANTHOLOGY

EDITED BY FREDERICK LUIS ALDAMA

DIARY OF A RELUCTANT DREAMER
By Alberto Ledesma

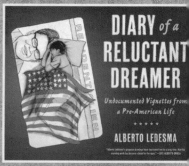

DIARY of a
RELUCTANT
DREAMER
Undocumented Vignettes from a Pre-American Life
★★★★★
ALBERTO LEDESMA

ANGELITOS
By Ilan Stavans & Santiago Cohen

A GRAPHIC NOVEL
ANGELITOS
ILAN STAVANS AND SANTIAGO COHEN